T0327895

**Compiled, edited and designed by
Damon Murray and Stephen Sorrell**

ALCOHOL
АЛКОГОЛЬ

FUEL

о мерах по преодо

on measures to ove

пьянства и ал

drinking and a

Alexei Plutser-Sarno

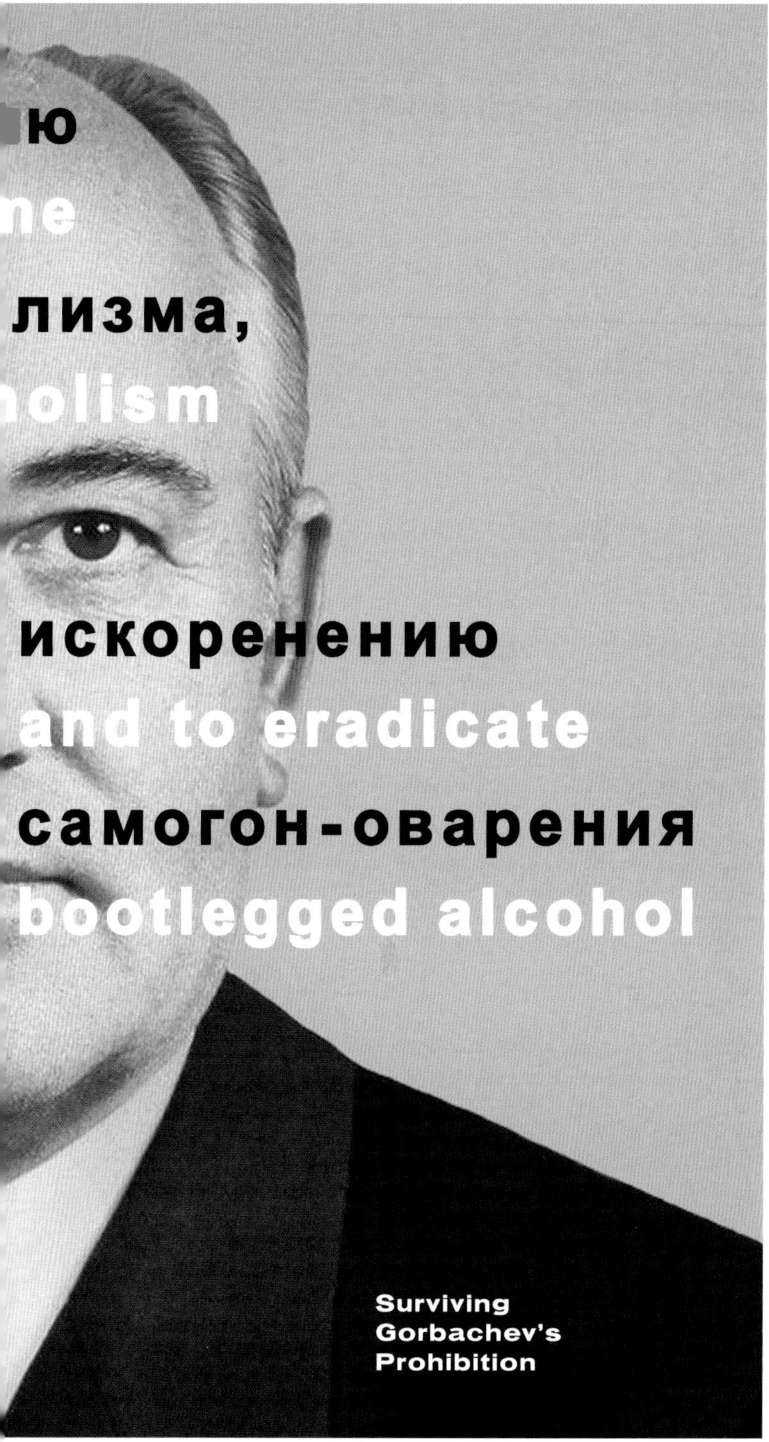

ю

ne

лизма,

nolism

искоренению

and to eradicate

самогон-оварения

bootlegged alcohol

On 11 March 1985, at the plenum of the Communist Party, Mikhail Gorbachev was elected General Secretary. With support from Mikhail Solomentsev and Yegor Ligachyov, he immediately initiated a new anti-alcohol drive, christened 'the Gorbachev campaign'.

A directive entitled 'On Measures to Overcome Drinking, Alcoholism and to Eradicate Bootlegged Alcohol' was issued on 7 May 1985. Hastily conceived and lacking sufficient planning or preparation, it was an attempt by the government to cut through a historic Gordian knot of social issues with little consideration for the consequences.

The campaign began by forcing the production lines of most of the distilleries and breweries to manufacture non-alcoholic drinks. This was swiftly followed by the closure of retail outlets selling alcohol. Around 80% of outlets across the Soviet Union were shut down; of the 1,500 'wine shops' in Moscow alone, only 150 were allowed to continue trading. In addition, the amount of wine an individual could buy at any one time was limited to two bottles. Weddings or funerals were the only exceptions, when up to ten bottles could be obtained – but only after the necessary paperwork had been presented to the salesperson. Non-alcoholic banquets and weddings were introduced, giving rise to the sarcastic slogan: 'March forward from a non-alcoholic wedding to an immaculate conception!'

Shops were permitted to sell alcohol only between 2pm and 7pm, so citizens would form queues early in the morning or even the night before. Crowded together in slow-moving lines, they grew bad-tempered and angry. Fights broke out and soon a police guard was required at even the smallest outlets.

The government crusade had a dramatic economic effect: according to Aleksandr Nemtsov at Moscow's Research Institute of Psychiatry, two and a half years into the campaign vodka sales had dropped by 63.6%. In 1985 citizens spent 5 billion rubles less on alcohol than in the previous year; in 1986 the drop in sales was 15.8 billion and in 1987 16.3 billion. In effect, government income had shrunk by more than 37 billion rubles. It was hoped that citizens' newly acquired spending power would be invested in consumer goods (food, clothes, footwear, etc.), but production levels failed to keep pace with the radical shift in the balance of supply and demand. To compound the problem, the shortfall in the availability of goods had a detrimental effect on the incentive to work: why bother, if there was nothing to buy?

In an attempt to minimise revenue losses, the government abruptly raised the price of alcohol. When Yuri Andropov was General Secretary, from 1982 to 1984, the cheapest brand of vodka cost 4.70 rubles a bottle. Just over two years later (August 1986) the price had increased to 9.10 rubles.

Ways were found to circumnavigate the prohibitions. Vodka could be bought at any time of day, at two or three times the official retail price, either from a cab driver (see p.177) or at a so-called 'drunk corner' (an illegal alcohol outlet). It could even be purchased at an official outlet outside the designated hours by paying double to the salesperson (see p.176).

Bootlegging proliferated, though the quality of home-made alcohol was vastly inferior to that of shop-bought brands. Distilled from various kinds of organic waste or cheap, sub-standard ingredients (starch, sugar, low-grade grains, rotten potatoes or beets), it was also often contaminated with large amounts of toxic fusel oils.

The authorities retaliated by ruling that the manufacture of wine and vodka would be punishable under criminal law, with anyone found guilty subject to a two-year prison sentence. In 1985 more than 100,000 people were charged with bootlegging, in 1986 over 200,000 and in 1987 nearly 400,000. By June 1987 the law had been mitigated: only those selling home-made alcohol would face prison while anyone producing alcohol for personal consumption escaped lightly (with administrative penalties, fines or public admonishment). At the same time, the government conducted a propaganda attack on bootleggers, presenting still-owners as enemies of the state and even as murderers.

On 1 July 1990 Gorbachev introduced alcohol coupons: each voucher could be exchanged for one bottle of vodka or two bottles of wine. This became the only way to buy these drinks. Unused vouchers would be collected from non-drinking relatives and friends and coupons were counterfeited and traded, becoming a currency in their own right. Later that year an additional quota was introduced for alcoholic beverages distributed through trades unions, with employees entitled to two bottles of vodka a month. The coupon system remained in place until the end of the Gorbachev era in December 1991.

From the alcohol recovery centre straight to gaol

Anyone found to be intoxicated would be picked up by the police and thrown into an alcohol recovery centre, with numbers increasing dramatically during the Gorbachev era. Citizens who had drunk even the smallest amount of alcohol – or who were simply out late at night – could find their freedom curtailed. Almost all detainees were held until the following morning. Police enthusiasm was easily explained: as well as covering the maintenance costs of the centres, revenue generated from fines provided bonuses for those who worked there.

The 'detoxification system' had originated not as a means of punishment but as a form of medical assistance. The first Russian facility, called 'The Shelter for the Inebriated', was opened in Tula on 7 November 1902 under the initiative of Fedor Arkhangelsky.

Alcoholics being treated under hypnosis at one of the psychiatric hospitals, scornfully referred to with the diminutive *psikushka*. These special hospitals were not run by the Ministry of Health, but by the Ministry of the Interior.

It employed a coachman to roam the city, picking up drunks who would otherwise have frozen to death on the streets and delivering them back to the safety of the shelter.

However, on 4 March 1940 People's Commissar Lavrentiy Beria issued Decree No. 00298, which transferred all detoxification facilities to the jurisdiction of the People's Commissariat for Internal Affairs (NKVD). Alcohol recovery centres soon became horrific prisons, a situation that continued throughout the Gorbachev era. On 30 May 1985 an ambiguous decree was issued stating that 'a medical detoxification facility… is a specialised militia establishment, administering preventative punishments for the breach of the anti-alcohol law, specifically for appearing intoxicated in public, and… providing first-aid and medical assistance to such individuals.' Over time fines reached the equivalent of half the average monthly wage and recovery centres became places where policemen robbed and assaulted detainees.

On 1 October 1985 the government decided to increase substantially the number of 'therapeutic-labour institutions' and the police and courts were granted the authority to consign offenders to these institutions, which in reality were more like prison camps. A letter of denunciation from a foreman or neighbour could be enough to sentence a person to two years. The government decree declared the need to 'develop a plan for the period 1986–90 for the construction and operation of therapeutic-labour institutions with autonomous manufacturing facilities accommodating 60,000 people.' With a single stroke of his pen, Gorbachev condemned to prison tens of thousands of citizens who had committed no crime. After completing a sentence, a record would be made in a citizen's labour book: for instance, 'LTP No.1. Underwent compulsory treatment and corrective labour for chronic alcoholism in Therapeutic-Labour Institution No.1 of the Department of Corrective-Labour Facilities of the Department of Internal Affairs of Kaluga Regional Committee.'

Of course, no actual treatment was offered. As in every other camp, 'rehabilitation' was to be achieved through an inexorable regime of backbreaking physical labour, starvation and freezing temperatures. Corruption among the wardens enabled the continuation of drinking among the inmates, who bought low-quality alcohol (primarily cheap colognes, methylated spirits and other ostensibly 'undrinkable' liquids) from their guards at extortionate prices. In the early 1980s around 150,000 drunks were detained in therapeutic-labour institutions.

Gorbachev then proceeded to create a network of 'hospitals' at plants and factories, where employees known to be alcohol-abusers were forced to live, working for a negligible fee. These 'patients', who received little treatment or therapy, were essentially slaves, with the government retaining 40% of their (already low) wages. Statistical data varies, but it is estimated that between 50,000 and 100,000 such 'slaves' were employed by various organisations during the Gorbachev era.

A decree issued by the Ministry of Health of the USSR on 25 June 1985 ordered the creation of 41,100 beds 'at industrial, agricultural, and construction-industry facilities'. Other organisations within the jurisdiction of these industries were authorised to create 11,520 more. In addition, a number of enterprises were permitted to expand their 'detoxification' prisons as required. Conditions – at factories, in fields or on construction sites – differed little from those in actual prisons. Moreover, if a 'slave' failed to fulfil an order given by a superior, he or she could expect to face a real prison term. Despite this threat, the free, unqualified workforce within the 'detoxification' facilities was completely ineffective.

Alcohol substitutes

Gorbachev visits the village where he was born. The locals throw a party in his honour and he is invited to have a drink with them. The next morning he wakes up with a horrific hangover. He looks at himself in the mirror and to his great surprise sees that the large birthmark on his forehead is gone.

'Comrades, what did we drink last night?' he asks.

'Well, we started with the two bottles of vodka you can get with coupons, then some denatured alcohol, then cologne, and when we ran out of perfume, we went on to stain remover.'

Mass consumption of alcohol surrogates began in the Gorbachev era. Of course, such behaviour had existed before, but now hundreds of thousands – perhaps even millions – of people were drinking substitute spirits. Tens of thousands of Soviet citizens died from poisoning each year.

These 'beverages' generally belonged to the following categories:

1. *Colognes*: perfumes, lotions, scented toilet waters, toothpastes, mouthwashes, haircare formulas, skin formulas, callus-removal treatments, foot deodorants, air fresheners (and many more).

2. *Chemicals*: glues, varnishes, denatured alcohol, polishes, cleaning products, car windscreen-washer fluids, grease removers, drain cleaners, medical-equipment disinfectants, solvents, alcohol-based mordants, anti-static sprays, brake fluids (known as 'undercarriage liqueur'), de-icers, insecticides (see p.123).

3. *Pharmacy*: medications and tinctures containing alcohol.

4. *Braga, brazhka*: home-made beverages of varying alcoholic content (usually between 3% and 7%) prepared by fermenting a

Triple
'An inexpensive toilet water for everyday use, with a fresh original odour. Indispensable for shaving.' Soviet perfume catalogue c.1980.

solution of sugar and yeast in water, sometimes with the addition of grains, malt, berries or honey. Braga has a fermentation period of approximately one week.

    5. *Moonshine*: home-made, low-quality vodka.

Colognes

In the 1980s the most popular group of non-codified liquids containing alcohol were lotions, which had fewer non-alcoholic additives and so were cheaper than colognes. The alcohol content of Soviet-made lotions ranged from 10% to 92.5% but most cheap brands contained around 35%. The two most commonly drunk were Cucumber (31%) and Rose Water (31%).

Sasha
'A complex and sophisticated eau de cologne. It is worthy of note that its odour is admired by the fair sex.' Soviet perfume catalogue c.1980.

Colognes were on average stronger – between 55% and 80% alcohol by volume. The most commonly drunk were Lilac (64%), Carnations (73%), Let's Go! (75%) and Triple (64%). Triple was also good value: in 1988 a 200ml bottle cost only 98 kopecks and a 100ml bottle 47 kopecks, whereas a bottle of vodka cost 10.20 rubles.

Vodka prices increased dramatically during the course of the anti-alcohol campaign. In 1981, Stolichnaya and Pshenichnaya vodkas were 6.20 rubles, rising to 7.20 rubles in 1985 and 10.20 in 1986. A worker's average monthly wage was still only 120 to 180 rubles – not enough to spend on vodka, even when it could be found in the shops.

However, empty vodka bottles could be returned for 20 kopecks each. Five empties, foraged from streets or dustbins, could secure a

bottle of Triple cologne with an intoxicating effect equal to 300ml of vodka. This made Triple the most popular alcoholic drink after moonshine. Nicknamed 'The Three Musketeers' or sometimes simply 'Dumas' (after the book's famous author), it was widely available from perfume counters and pharmacies. Triple was also regularly smuggled into prisons hidden inside convicts' parcels. A mixture of Triple and Sasha colognes was nicknamed 'Emperor Aleksandr III' (mimicking cognacs such as Henri IV, Louis XIII and Napoleon; Sasha is a diminutive form of Aleksandr).

The state manufactured some 700 varieties of scented products in line with GOST National Standards. These included the following brands of cologne, listed in order of decreasing aroma and price (colognes in Group C were most often consumed orally as they were both the cheapest and the least poisonous):

1. Group A, containing no less than 70% alcohol by volume: The Eighth of March, The Tale of Czar Saltan, Dnepro, Lel, Anniversary, Firyuza, Aurora Borealis, The Lilac of Riga, Dear Kharkov, Youth, Red Poppy, Magnolia, Lavender Extra, Smoke, Shipr.

2. Group B, containing no less than 60% alcohol by volume: Beacon Lights, Spring Brooks, Lemon, Grapes, Staccato, Little Flower, Little Gnome, Sainis, Staburadze, Lauma, The New, Let's Go!, Moidodyr, Extra Hygienic, Pavasaris, Good Morning!, Russian Forest.

3. Group C, containing no less than 55% alcohol by volume: Lilac, Refreshing, Triple and others.

Initially people drank colognes simply because they did not have enough money to buy vodka. Gradually, however, colognes became

above: **Russian Forest**
'The subtle pine aroma reminds one of a pine forest in winter. It will satisfy the requirements of the most fastidious customer. A round bottle of thin glass with a fur-branch pattern.' Soviet perfume catalogue c.1980.

left: **Crystal**
'This clean, fresh scent enjoys well-deserved popularity and is presented in an exquisite crystal-shaped bottle.' Soviet perfume catalogue c.1980.

the 'drink of the people', acquiring their own culture, myths and symbolic associations, based on characteristics such as brand names. As Venedikt Yerofeyev writes in his semi-autobiographical postmodernist prose-poem *Moscow-Petushki* ('Moscow to the End of the Line', 1969–70): 'Silver Lily of the Valley is not the same as White Lilac in its moral aspect, let alone in its bouquet. Lily of the Valley, for instance, agitates the mind, disturbs the consciousness and strengthens a sense of justice.' Names such as Silver Lily of the Valley have sentimental connotations, while Lel – a reference to a Slavic god of love and marriage mentioned in Pushkin's poem 'Ruslan and Ludmila' – brings a touch of romance. Other names such as Good Morning! sound comical, while Russian Forest invokes patriotic thoughts. The leaflets accompanying the colognes were a source of amusement to drinkers. The blurb for Lavender face lotion, for instance, claimed it was good for your health, with its ingredients listed as Vitamin C, natural lavender oil and 35% alcohol: 'It cleanses, has antiseptic properties, and gives your skin a healthy, fresh look.'

From 1987 to 1988 I was a member of a work brigade in which half the workers drank a bottle of cologne (usually Triple, Sasha or Masha) or two bottles of lotions (mostly Cucumber or Rose Water) every day. Mouthwashes were similarly popular. BF glue was also used, though since this required a special purification process it was consumed rarely and by only three workers. According to our calculations, in a year our brigade drank about 1,000 bottles of cologne and up to 3,000 vials of lotion and mouthwash. BF glue was consumed about once a week, so three workers drank some 100 containers of glue (each 100ml) per year. A small bag of sweets or a lump of sugar would serve as a chaser for the colognes and chemicals.

Perfume was expensive and so was not bought for drinking – though it was sometimes 'borrowed' if left unattended, to be used as a hair of the dog. The following brands of perfume were manufactured in the USSR: Youth, Crystal, White Lilac, Magnolia, Talisman, Shipr, Tender, The Fountain of Bakhchysarai, The Caucasus, Desires, Turaidas Roze, Vizbulite, The Lilac of Riga, Diamond, Mask, Sapphire, Camomile, A Winter Evening (among others).

In addition, cheap skin conditioners, foot remedies and anti-dandruff formulas were consumed. Certain mouthwashes were alcohol based, with an ethanol content of between 20% and 30%; Mint, Extra and Dew were widely used for drinking.

Chemicals

Methylated spirit and denatured alcohol were the most popular of the chemical alcohol substitutes. *The Soviet Encyclopedic Dictionary* defines methylated spirit as: 'ethanol that contains additives, such as dyes, giving it a purple colour. Used as a thinner for lacquers and finishes, it has an extremely bad taste and smell. Toxic.' Denatured alcohol is defined as 'a translucent liquid with a strong, unpleasant odour, made from the by-products of alcohol manufacture… It is intended for technical use only and is bottled in containers ranging from 0.5 to 30 litres.' Pyridine, acetone, acetic acid, methanol and other additives are used to turn ethanol into denatured alcohol; different varieties have an alcohol content of between 85% and 95%. According to the *Soviet Encyclopedic Dictionary*, 'Denatured alcohol must be labelled "poison".'

Methylated spirit was sold in pharmacies, but it was also shipped to factories in industrial quantities for use in their products or processes and was almost exclusively consumed on these premises (see p.96). It would often be mixed with other drinks: a combination of denatured alcohol with beer was called chernoburka (silver fox). Cheap, light draft beer, in ratios of 1:1 to 1:5 of alcohol to beer, was the usual mixer.

Varnishes were similarly popular. A varnish is a '10–20% solution of natural resins in alcohol… when applied to wooden surfaces it creates a clear coating' (*Soviet Encyclopedic Dictionary*). Varnishes were widely used in factories, where they were consumed in such large quantities that during the Gorbachev era varnish became a national drink of sorts. Between 100ml and 300ml of undiluted varnish would constitute a 'serving' for one person. Varnish drinkers were colloquially referred to as 'aubergines' because their skin acquired a purple hue.

Lacquers were not consumed neat and required some preparation, which made them less popular. Alcohol-based lacquers are '30–40% resin solution, in 90–95% alcohol. The film-forming agents of alcohol-based lacquers are natural resins (shellac, soft copal, sandarac, mastic, rosin, acaroid resin), as well as synthetic phenol aldehyde resins. To increase the film's elasticity, alcohol-based lacquers are softened with castor oil and fatty acids obtained from flaxseed oil' (*Soviet Encyclopedic Dictionary*). Before drinking, a lacquer should be 'cleaned' using a method involving table salt and water (see below). The resulting solution contains ethanol with a number of admixtures.

BF glue was also widely used by factory workers. BF stands for 'Bakelite Phenolic', defined by the *Soviet Encyclopedic Dictionary* as a 'synthetic compound used for joining different materials by means of an adhesive bond between the layer of glue and the surfaces of the materials to be bonded.' BF-2, BF-3 and BF-4 were used industrially, while BF-6 was employed for medical purposes to close wounds. The 'Register of Medicines' describes it as, 'Phenol polyvinyl acetate glue… an alcohol solution of phenol formaldehyde resin, polyvinyl butyral, and rosin… Pharmacological effect: isolating, wound healing, antiseptic. For external application only. Distributed in 15g glass containers.' Colloquially, BF glue was known as Boris Fyodorovich after the 16th-century Czar Boris Fyodorovich Gudunov.

Like lacquers, glues require preliminary refining before consumption. The conventional procedure involved mixing 200ml of glue, 300ml of water and 10g of table salt. This solution was then shaken for fifteen minutes; at a factory or plant, mixing could be accelerated by using a power drill. The process separated the glue into a solid resin 'sediment' and 500g of milky drinkable liquid (30% alcohol) with a strong odour.

Alcohol-based hydraulic fluid (brake fluid) was also widely consumed. It was intended for use in hydraulic braking and gear-shifting systems and those who worked with it were advised to 'wear rubber gloves and protective goggles. Keep away from open fire. Prevent contact with skin or eyes. If contact occurs, flush with plenty of water. Seek immediate medical attention' (Soviet-era instruction manual for the handling of hydraulic fluids). Diluted aviation brake fluid, known colloquially as 'undercarriage liqueur', contained ethanol and glycerin alongside other components.

Insecticides would be sprayed from the can directly into a glass of beer, in two or three short bursts, then drunk immediately. Air fresheners, also in aerosol cans, had to be purified if they were to be consumed in large quantities. A small hole would be punched in the can with a nail; between ten and fifteen minutes later all the pressurised gas would have escaped, allowing the can to be cut open. The contents would then be poured out and allowed to rest for an hour, after which salt and water were added. Once the sediment was removed the potion would be ready to drink.

In their zeal to eradicate alcoholism, party bureaucrats issued directives for the mandatory replacement of ethanol with methanol – a lethal alcohol – in a number of chemicals. This resulted in the death of tens of thousands of habitual chemical drinkers who were unaware of the substitution. Gorbachev was informed of the tragic consequences of the policy but seemed indifferent; in his book *Memoirs* (1996) he blamed his lack of remedial action on a full itinerary and a desire for discretion: 'I heard rumours that the situation had deviated off course; reliable sources drew my attention to that fact. But my extremely busy schedule caused an avalanche of other problems, and my inner sense of tact, if you will, got in the way.'

Gorbachev also brought the might of the anti-alcohol campaign to bear on the armed forces, with the result that the military too switched en masse to alcohol substitutes. Enquiries were made at the highest levels, alcoholics were hunted out in military districts and garrisons, celebrations of promotions and periods of leave were banned. Denouncement flourished. Official vodka coupons were often withheld because commanders declared that no one in their garrison drank. As a result, the consumption of moonshine and denatured alcohol became commonplace.

Airforce ground crew would drain the de-icing fluid from aircraft, distill it, and then drink it. They often covered up their theft by the dangerous practice of replacing the de-icing fluid with water: if the de-icing tanks had to be used at high altitudes, the water would freeze on the wings and almost certainly result in a crash. The alcohol used in cooling and braking systems was particularly valued, not just because it was free, but also because it was purer than commercially available alcohol; it became known as 'white gold' because of its great value on the black market.

Pharmacy

A further category of non-codified drinks, colloquially known as 'pharmacy', consisted of medications containing ethanol. The consumption of these preparations was as widespread as that of colognes or chemicals. The most popular medications are listed below:

1. *Tinctures* (solutions of alcohol and water containing animal, vegetable or chemical drugs): Capsicum (1:10) in a 90% alcohol solution; Valocordin (1:5) in a 90% alcohol solution; peony (1:10) in a 40% alcohol solution; St. John's wort (1:5) in a 40% alcohol solution; valerian root (1:5) in a 70% alcohol solution; ginseng (1:10) in a 70% alcohol solution; marigold (1:10) in a 70% alcohol solution; eucalyptus (1:5) in a 70% alcohol solution.

2. *Extracts*: Siberian ginseng root (1:1) in a 50% alcohol solution; pantocrin (a Siberian stag-antler extract) in a 50% alcohol solution.

3. *Medicinal*: 'juices' such as aloe vera, containing aloe 80ml, ethanol 20ml.

The financial logic that ruled the consumption of cologne also applied to 'pharmacy' drinks. In 1988 a 50ml bottle of capsicum tincture could be purchased for 17 kopecks in any pharmacy; some eight to ten of these bottles contained the same volume of alcohol as a bottle of vodka. However, vodka was extremely difficult to find and cost about 10 rubles a bottle whereas 500ml of readily available tincture cost only 1.70 rubles.

Braga, brazhka and moonshine

'In the window stands a plastic jug filled with murky liquid, its neck sealed with a rubber glove that seems to be waving hello. "That's how you know it's ready," Zhbanov says. "The gas released from fermentation makes the glove inflate. We call that the Hitler salute".' (Simon Shuster, *Time* magazine, 9 May 2011)

For most of the 20th century brazhka was made almost exclusively from water, yeast and sugar. During the course of the anti-alcohol campaign, however, the sugar needed to make both moonshine and brazhka disappeared from shops – along with colognes, lotions and even some toothpastes. When produced in the home, brazhka is usually fermented in a standard jar with a rubber glove pulled over the open top. As fermentation takes place the glove slowly fills with gas. Finally, when the process is complete, it stands upright in silent salute. At the time of the anti-alcohol campaign this type of brazhka was ironically known as 'Hello to Gorbachev'; today it is usually referred to as 'Heil Hitler!'

In a work environment brazhka was often fermented in a fire extinguisher to keep it hidden from the administration. Once the contents of the extinguisher had been emptied out and the inside cleaned, it could be hung back on the wall without causing suspicion. Milk churns and gas canisters also made perfect camouflage for fermenting brazhka. In garages or fabrication workshops such containers could conceal their alcoholic content while remaining in plain sight.

Drinking like a man

The notion that drinks should be 'bitter', unpleasant, unpalatable and difficult to swallow is widespread in Russia, hence the expression: 'We drink a lot, but with a great deal of disgust.' Even drunks view drinking as suffering – a form of self-flagellation, an ascetic renouncement of pleasure or voluntary martyrdom. In Russia sweetened drinks are considered suitable only for women; a 'real man' consumes only bitter drinks (including vodka).

The 'heroic' drinkers of the Gorbachev era had to find places where they could pursue their habits in peace. All public drinking establishments were closed and punishments meted out by the police made it dangerous to drink substitute substances in public places. Toilets, train carriages, entrances to apartment blocks, attics and basements became preferred locations for alcohol consumption. Of course, these places had been used for drinking before, but never on such a scale.

From 1985 to 1987 sales of BF glue increased by 26%, window cleaners by 13%, insecticides by 15% and colognes and lotions by 29%. Before the campaign the USSR manufactured over 100,000 tons of perfume annually; approximately half of that was used for drinking during each year of the Gorbachev era. In 1987 alone, the estimated death toll from the consumption of the substances listed above was 11,000.

Failure as success

A young boy and his father walk past an alcohol outlet with a very long queue. The boy looks at the people in the line, dumbfounded, and asks: 'Dad, who are these people?'

'Those are loafers, son. They're too lazy to build a still for themselves.'

The pinnacle of political folly was Gorbachev's decision to destroy all the country's vineyards and so eradicate its wine-making industry.

In total, approximately half of all Soviet vineyards were lost; Moldavia alone suffered the destruction of some 80,000 hectares of high-quality vines. Yegor Ligachyov, Gorbachev's closest ally and an instigator of the campaign, ordered that the vineyards of the famous Massandra winery in the Crimea be destroyed; the winery was closed and much of its unique collection, which included samples of every wine produced there in the last hundred years, was ransacked. After failing to dissuade Gorbachev from tearing down the Magarach wine-making and research centre, the institute's director, Professor Pavel Golodriga, committed suicide. Plantations of hops and high-quality barley, necessary for the production of beer malt, suffered a similar fate. The vineyards have never been fully re-established.

A more absurd Party decision mandated the censorship of scenes of wine-drinking within works of art. According to a directive issued by the Central Committee of the Communist Party on 7 May 1985, 'Any instances when the "cultural" moderate consumption of alcoholic beverages is promoted, or feast and drinking rituals are depicted in a positive light, are completely inadmissible, in both mass media and works of art, in film or television.' The Party proceeded to cut any such scenes from films, publications and performances. Banned works included Isaak Dunayevsky's 'Waltz Zazdravnaya' from the 1936 film *The Circus*; Modest Mussorgsky's 19th-century opera *Boris Godunov*; Ludwig van Beethoven's *Twenty-Five Scottish Songs* (1818); 'The Drinking Song' from Giuseppe Verdi's 1853 opera *La traviata*, and hundreds of others.

The anti-alcohol campaign was also economically flawed. Before 1985 alcohol sales had accounted for between 30% and 40% of budget revenue but by 1987 food-industry receipts had dropped by almost 50%, from 60 billion to 35 billion rubles. The campaign was a key contributor to the 1987 economic crisis. After five years of Gorbachev's leadership, economic growth went into reverse – from 2.3% to -11% – the value of gold reserves depreciated tenfold, foreign-exchange reserves fifteenfold, the dollar-to-ruble exchange rate tumbled from 60 kopecks to 90 rubles per dollar and the national debt grew by 500%. However, just as analysts had predicted, Soviet drinkers did not stop drinking but simply switched to homemade alcohol and alcohol surrogates. Instead of putting a stop to alcohol abuse, Gorbachev had wrecked the economy of the Soviet Union.

Gorbachev proceeded to report the failure of the campaign as a success, declaring in 1989: 'We took it upon ourselves to eliminate drinking and alcoholism… We initiated healthy processes in economy, politics, ideology, culture – everywhere.' In later interviews he attempted to extricate himself from the consequences of his decisions, blaming his comrades and the system instead.

Ostensibly the anti-alcohol campaign collapsed on 1 January 1988 when the Council of Ministers of the USSR issued a decree that increased – by a small amount – the government-controlled manufacture and distribution of spirits. On 25 October the Central Committee issued a directive entitled 'On the Progress of Fulfillment of the Decree of the Central Committee of the Communist Party on Intensifying the Measures against Drinking and Alcoholism'. This officially marked the failure, and end, of the campaign.

The results of Gorbachev's anti-alcohol campaign were the disintegration of the country's economy and the mass drinking that followed. According to official statistics alone, consumption of spirits in Russia grew by 233% between 1988 and 1998. If the consumption of bootlegged and surrogate alcohol is taken into account, the figure is much higher. By way of comparison, in Italy consumption of alcohol during the same period dropped by 50%, in Belgium by 28% and in Switzerland and Britain by 27%. Repercussions from actions initiated during this period continued to unfold for years to come. Even today, the practice of consuming surrogate alcohol remains firmly rooted in society.

Photographs: Vladimir Sichov. Moscow, mid-1970s.

overleaf:

Fight bootlegging!

Annually, around 200,000,000 puds* of bread is used for making alcohol. Converted into money, this accounts for 140,000,000 rubles.

With this kind of money, one could

Open 96,000 schools or 233,000 reading izbas†
Buy 11,000,000 ploughs or 700,000 reapers.
Buy 2,800,000 cows or 1,400,000 horses.
Buy 400 million arshins‡ of chintz.

Bootlegging devastates peasant farms,
destroys a man's health, kills him, and leads to crimes.

* A pud is around 16.8 kg.
† Izba, a peasant's log house.
‡ Arshin is 710 cm.

Artist unknown, c.1921
580 x 850 mm

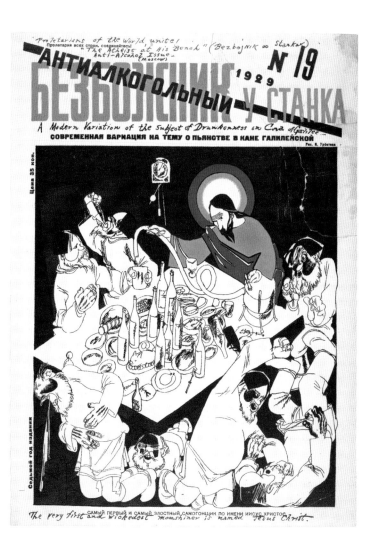

Proletarians of the world unite!
The Atheist at his bench.

A modern variation of the subject of drunkenness in Cana of Galilee.

The very first and persistent moonshiner named Jesus Christ.

Bezbozhnik (Godless), 1929
Atheist magazine, anti-alcohol issue, 310 x 230 mm

НА БОРЬБУ

САМОГОНЩИНА РАЗО
РАЗРУШАЕТ ЗДОРОВЬЕ ЧЕЛОВЕКА, ГУБ

Агитационное Отделение Главполитпросвета. Изд-ство „Долой Неграмотность". Кузнецкий пер. д. 4.

САМОГОНОМ!

На самогон тратится в год около 200.000.000 пудов хлеба-в переводе на деньги-140.000.000 руб.

ЧТО МОЖНО СДЕЛАТЬ НА ЭТИ ДЕНЬГИ

ОТКРЫТЬ ШКОЛ	КУПИТЬ ПЛУГОВ	КОРОВ	СИТЦУ
96.000	11.000.000	2.800.000	
ИЛИ ИЗБ-ЧИТАЛЕН	ИЛИ ЖНЕЕК	ИЛИ ЛОШАДЕЙ	
233.000	700.000	1.400.000	400 МИЛЛ. АРШИН

КРЕСТЬЯНСКОЕ ХОЗЯЙСТВО, ...ТОМСТВО и ВЕДЕТ К ПРЕСТУПЛЕНИЯМ

Главлит № 29672. Тираж 30.000.   Военная Типография Управления РККА, Знаменка, д. 23.

He didn't have much...

Not a single drop!

No!

Artist unknown, 1963
Matchbox labels,
45 x 35 mm

Arrows, top to bottom: **Illness, Absenteeism, Prison**

Text on the bottle reads: **Vodka**

The shadows of the past.

pages 29–32:
Artist unknown, 1956
Matchbox labels, 50 x 35 mm

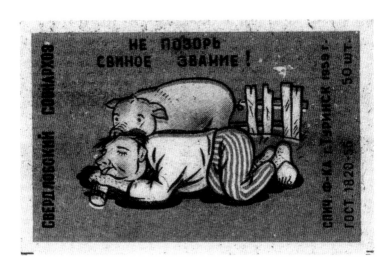

Do not disgrace the status of a pig!

A villain with a label.

Text on the bottle reads: **Vodka**

Enough drinking!

Wine and brains don't mix.

He drank vodka –
And drowned himself.

Drinking leads to no good.

Daddy, don't drink.

D. Bulanov, 1929
420 x 295 mm

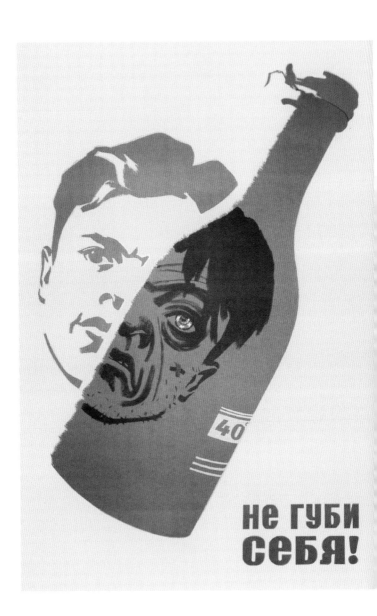

Don't wreck yourself!

V. Briskin, 1963
630 x 440 mm

Ivan Ivanovich was heading home,
With a paycheck in his pocket…
He met a friend in the pub,
And turned into a dog.

Text above the window reads: **Pay window**

I. Astapov, 1962
567 x 430 mm

A drunk out hunting is a criminal.

V. Kireev, c.1960
440 x 600 mm

right:
He drinks vodka and wine,
And gets drunk every day.
The results are obvious –
He's the reason we fall short of our target.

B. Rezanov, 1963
430 x 330 mm

ХЛЕЩЕТ ВОДКУ И ВИНЦО,
ЧТО НИ ДЕНЬ, ТО ПЬЯН.
РЕЗУЛЬТАТЫ — НАЛИЦО:
ОН СРЫВАЕТ ПЛАН!

Художник Б. Рофанов
Отмач Ю. Юрова

37

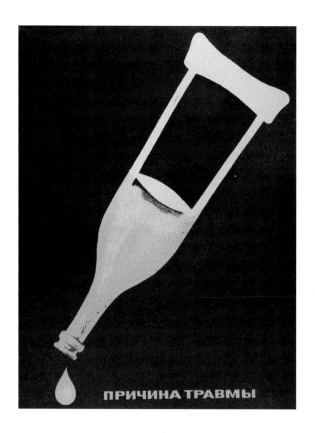

ПРИЧИНА ТРАВМЫ

The cause of injuries.

V. Kireev, 1977
600 x 420 mm

right:
He'll do anything to get a drink.
He'll steal public property.

Let's board up this hole in the fence.
We won't tolerate a drunk and a thief!

Text on the bucket reads: **Linseed oil**

B. Rezanov, 1964
355 x 255 mm

ЧТОБ НАПИТЬСЯ, ОН НА ВСЕ ИДЕТ,
ОН ДОБРО НАРОДНОЕ КРАДЕТ...

ЗАКОЛОТИМ ЭТУ ЩЕЛЬ ЗАБОРА!
НЕ ПОТЕРПИМ ПЬЯНИЦУ И ВОРА!

ОЛИФА

His motto: Put all efforts
Into making easy money.
A flier is a typical parasite.
He's the one pulling us down.

Text on the book reads: **Employment Record**
The name underneath reads: **P. Fly-by-night**

Y. Kershin, 1983
430 550 mm

right:
We'll kick out the drunks
From the working masses.
– Vladimir Mayakovsky

Text on the pipe reads: **Rejects**
Text on the bottle reads: **Vodka**

V. Govorkov, 1966
328 x 240 mm

Brought to the Hospital...

Text on the bottle reads: **Vodka**

V. Glivenko, Ukrainian SSR, 1962
290 x 460 mm

ЛІКАРНЯ

Довела...

БФ 36685 11.IX.62 р. Зам. 1148. Тираж 3000.
Ф-ка офсетного друку Головполіграфвидаву
Міністерства культури УРСР м. Київ, вул. Фрунзе, 51-а
Ціна 4 коп.

Alcohol does not make you
happy, it destroys your health.

A blood test can cost
you your licence.

Alcohol at the workplace
reduces alertness.

Don't race with them,
they'll outrun you.

pages 44–45:
Artist unknown, Czechoslovakia, 1959
Matchbox labels, 50 x 35 mm

Once you quit drinking, you
can furnish your apartment.

If you give in,
it will enslave you.

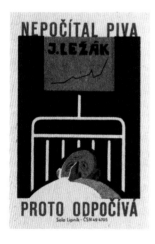

Lost count of your beer?
Now you get to rest.

On the chart: **J. Ležák***

* This reads like a name, but the
word ležák also means 'lager beer'
and 'bedridden patient'.

Alcohol drowns wishes
and desires.

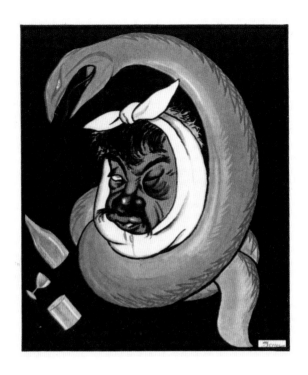

V. Deni, 1932
330 x 390 mm

right:
On the snake are various labels from alcoholic drinks.

Not among trees or grasses,
The serpent has warmed up among us.

Don't suck on him, mammals,
Or you'll turn into a reptile yourself.

A. E. Bazilevich, Ukrainian SSR, 1972
872 x 580 mm

Не в пущах повз, не в осоці,—
Пригрівсь горілич-змій між нами.

Ви не смокчіть його, „ссавці“,
Бо й вас поробить плазунами

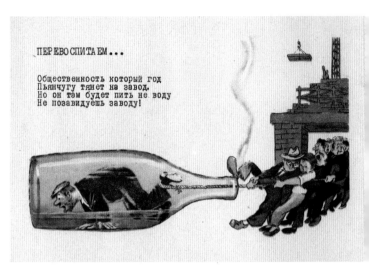

ПЕРЕВОСПИТАЕМ...

Общественность который год
Пьянчугу тянет на завод,
Но он там будет пить не воду
Не позавидуешь заводу!

We will reform him...

The community has been trying for years,
To bring this drunk back to work.
But what he's going to drink there is not going to be water.
The factory's situation will not be something to envy.

D. Oboznenko, 1976
Newspaper cartoon, 100 x 160 mm

She stole him away...

He drank on his payday; he drank on Saturdays,
Said he was spending his own money after all.
Before he knew it,
He traded his family for vodka.

Text on the bottle reads: **Vodka**

E. Rabinovich, 1976
Newspaper cartoon, 115 x 160 mm

'How can I go to work?'

His weakness for wine,
Made him a prisoner of the bottle.

Artist unknown, 1980s
Newspaper cartoon, 115 x 160 mm

Lost both his family and his health.

Text on the bottle reads: **Vodka**

P. Letunov, 1982
550 x 430 mm

Either, or.

Text on the bottle reads: **Vodka**

P. Letunov, 1983
400 x 550 mm

Make sure your construction site is free of professional drunkards!

Text on the bottle reads: **Vodka**

A. L. Braz, 1972
1000 x 670 mm

We will be resolute in fighting shirkers, bunglers, and scroungers!

Text on figures reads: **Shirker, Embezzler, Bungler**
The label attached to blue figure reads: **Rejects**

V. Kononov, 1983
660 x 480 mm

Alcohol is evil!

This leads to disaster!

Alcohol is nature's pain!

Artists unknown, pocket calendar, 1984
100 x 70 mm

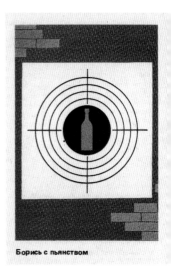

Fight against drinking.

Drunkenness won't be tolerated!

The headings on the papers inside the vodka bottle read: **13th month salary, sanatorium voucher, bonus**

Artist unknown, c.1986
660 x 480 mm

This shine is not going
to adorn a table.
The halo is all too gloomy.

V. I. Sobruk, 1982
420 x 290 mm

Squanderers and thieves,
everybody with a guilty
conscience, cannot
escape the vigilant eyes
of the Komsomol*
Watch Brigade.

* Komsomol was the
All-Union Leninist Young
Communist League

V. Konovalov, 1960s
1270 x 790 mm

**Thanks to my mummy and daddy,
I'm not deprived of anything!**

T. A. Lyashchuk, Ukrainian SSR, 1984
840 x 620 mm

Everywhere, every drunken hoodlum will be decisively repulsed!

Artist unknown, c.1986
338 x 263 mm

A slippery slope...

Text on the stairs reads:
**Banquet
Drinking
Absenteeism
Disorderly Conduct
Crime**

Artist unknown, c.1986
352 x 264 mm

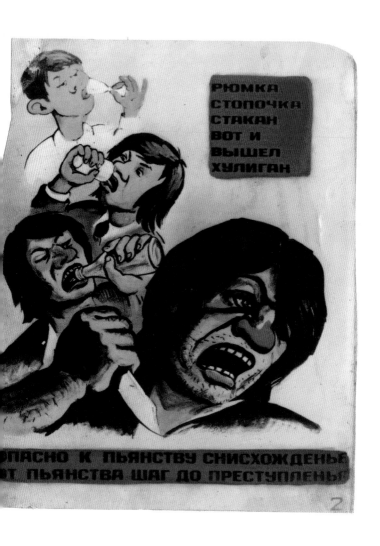

РЮМКА
СТОПОЧКА
СТАКАН
ВОТ И
ВЫШЕЛ
ХУЛИГАН

ПАСНО К ПЬЯНСТВУ СНИСХОЖДЕНЬЕ
Т ПЬЯНСТВА ШАГ ДО ПРЕСТУПЛЕНЬЯ

Little by little, and you end up with a hooligan.

Tolerance of drinking is dangerous.
There is but a step from drinking to crime.

Artist unknown, c.1986
325 x 260 mm

**Special clothes, or overalls
can't disguise alcohol.
Don't try to get it into the workshop –
Don't slip it past security!**

Text above the entrance reads:
Checkpoint

Initials on the red sleeve read:
NK (*Narodny Kontrol*, 'People's Supervision').

A. Ordinartsev, 1981
430 x 270 mm

**НИ В СПЕЦОВКУ, НИ В РОБУ
НЕ РЯДИСЬ, АЛКОГОЛЬ.
В ЦЕХ ПРОБРАТЬСЯ НЕ ПРОБУЙ—
НЕ ПРОПУСТИТ КОНТРОЛЬ!**

Художник А. ОРДИНАРЦЕВ, стихи В. ПОЛУЯНА

Подп. в печать 17.11.80. А-12202. Формат 60×90/₁₆. П. л. 1. Усл. п. л. 3. Изд.
№ 14в-4. Тираж 193000 экз. Цена 4 коп.
© Издательство «Плакат», 1981 г.

In memory of those who have fallen in
the struggle against casual drinking
and alcoholism.

Artist unknown, 1987
872 x 580 mm

overleaf:
It is criminally reckless to introduce
the young to alcohol.

M. I. Heifits, 1970
438 x 568 mm

'A polyglot'*

His pallette is rather broad,
from kerosene to varnishes.
And no one has been able to figure out so far,
How to talk sense into such a... 'connoisseur'!

* A pun as the word polyglot sounds like glutton to 'uneducated' people. Glot is similar to glotat 'to gobble up' or 'to swallow'.

V. Kyunnap, 1985
440 x 330 mm

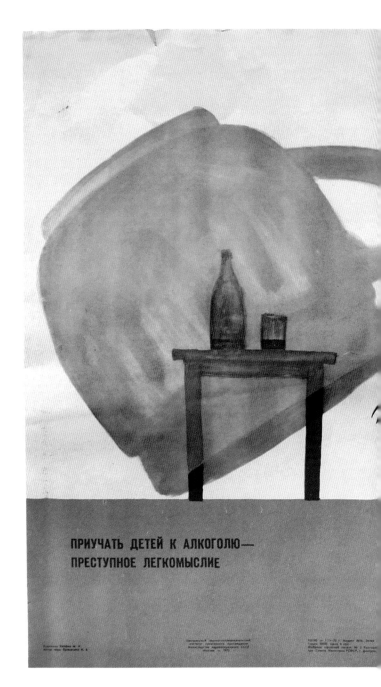

ПРИУЧАТЬ ДЕТЕЙ К АЛКОГОЛЮ—
ПРЕСТУПНОЕ ЛЕГКОМЫСЛИЕ

**Where there is vodka
there is crime.**

L. Kuharuk, 1988
550 x 430 mm

I. Tarasov, 1988
550 x 430 mm

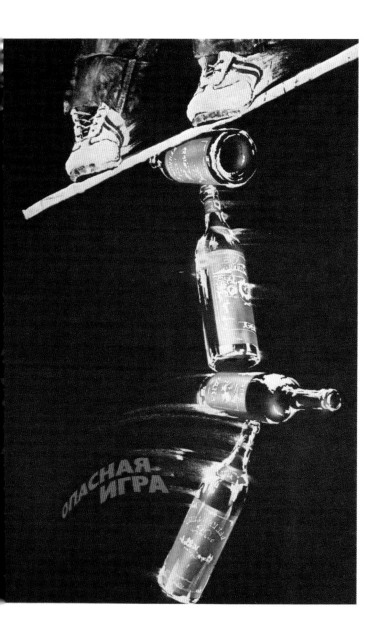

A dangerous game.

G. Popesku, 1988
550 x 430 mm

Handwritten note reads:
Daddy, don't drink!

Sign behind reads:
The Wine Shop
Opening hours
Saturday
Sunday: closed

V. Balashov, 1985   V. Maer, 1985
550 x 430 mm   550 x 430 mm

A. Ratomsky, 1988
600 x 430 mm

Sobriety is the law of the road.

O. Domanova, A. Domanov, 1988
550 x 430 mm

It starts small.

O. Belov, 1988
550 x 430 mm

A dangerous pattern: knock it out!

Pictured is a 'figure' (or 'pattern') from the game of *gorodki*, a variation of the game of skittles. The objective is to throw a wooden bat at a set of wooden pegs or skittles that are arranged in certain patterns or 'figures', and knock them out of a square zone in which they are arranged. The figure pictured here is called 'the machine gun installation'.

E. Burlov, 1988
550 x 430 mm

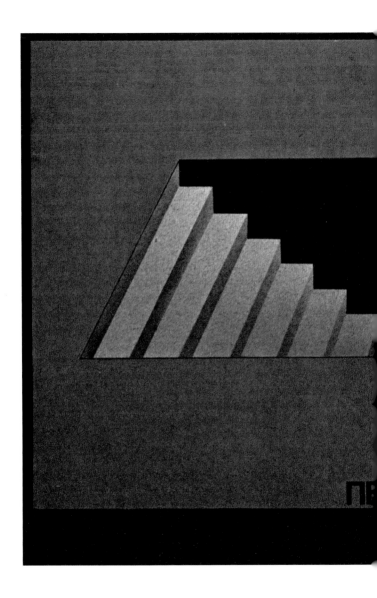

UNDERPASS – to the 'next world'.

S. Smirnov, 1988
430 x 550 mm

Protect nature from 'barbarians'!

A. Tanel, 1985
420 x 550 mm

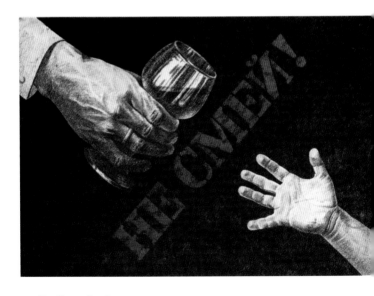

Don't you dare!

V. Maer, 1985
420 x 550 mm

Alco*hol*

The pun is formed by artificially breaking the word алкоголь (alcohol) into two parts: алко (alcoholic) and голь (the poor, beggars).

R. Akmanov, 1988
550 x 430 mm

Художник П. Д. Егоров

© Политиздат Украины, 1987

We'll sweep them out!

P. D. Yegorov, Ukrainian SSR, 1987
434 x 280 mm

To your sort, we say: 'Enough! There's no place for you at the plant!'

Text in the top right dust cloud reads: **Rejects**

O. K. Kohan, Ukrainian SSR, 1986
585 x 410 mm

Honour, Family, Work, Health.

He befriended the bottle and fell into an abyss.

V. O. Pashenko, Ukrainian SSR, 1979
440 x 290 mm

This is a shameful union – a slacker + vodka!

V. O. Pashenko, Ukrainian SSR, 1981
440 x 290 mm

**If you had too much while carousing,
you'll have too little productivity.**

Diagonal text in the percentage sign reads: **Of the quota**

V. O. Pashenko, Ukrainian SSR, 1981
440 x 290 mm

Once there was a person...

E. L. Kudryashov, Ukrainian SSR, 1981
440 x 290 mm

**It twisted and pulled him and finally did him in.
We need to root out this evil!**

V. M. Reshetov, Ukrainian SSR, 1980
440 x 290 mm

Vodka

E. L. Kudryashov, Ukrainian SSR, 1981
440 x 290 mm

QUOTA
Ful/filled

**The lazy bum is undermining our quota.
And we busy ourselves with him. Why?**

V. M. Reshetov, Ukrainian SSR, 1980
440 x 290 mm

НА ФАБРИЦІ Й ФЕРМІ, НА ПОЛІ Й ЗАВОДІ
ТАКИМ МИ РІШУЧЕ ГОВОРИМО: ГОДІ!

**At a factory and on a farm, in the field and at the plant,
To the likes of you we resolutely say: Enough!**

V. M. Reshetov, Ukrainian SSR, 1984
440 x 290 mm

Rowdy partying ends in a bitter hangover.

Text on the tattoo reads: **I love order**

V. O. Pashenko, Ukrainian SSR, 1985
440 x 290 mm

overleaf:
Exercise equals health! This is the only way!

P. Sabinin, 1988
480 x 650 mm

ГУЧНЕ ДОЗВІЛЛЯ—ГІРКЕ ПОХМІЛЛЯ

Физкультура – зд

ТОЛЬКО ТА

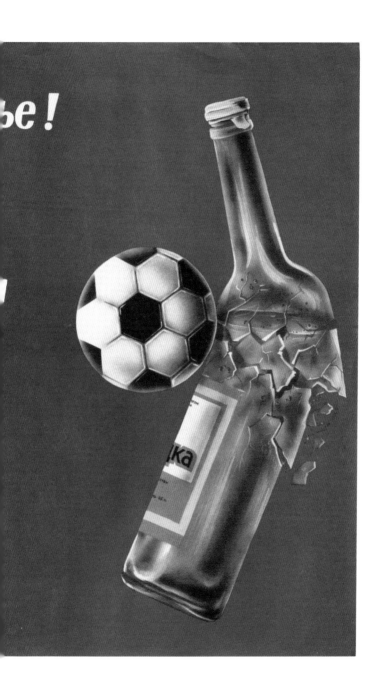

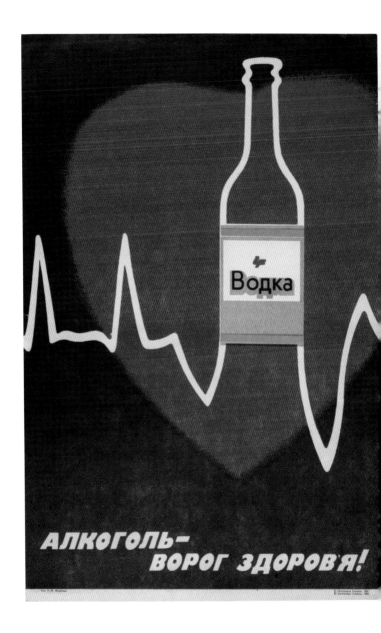

Alcohol is bad for your health!

T. M. Fomichova, Ukrainian SSR, 1981
440 x 295 mm

Drink – to lose!

R. S. Akmaev, 1988
875 x 580 mm

We won't let it happen!

Artist unknown, 1986
550 x 427 mm

Drunkenness won't be tolerated.

E. S. Hepanchuk, 1985
420 x 300 mm

For the degreasing of parts.

Drunks seemingly have no shame,
They are unlikely to start the workday.
Their only dream is to drink some ethanol at public's expense,
The rest are details.

Text on the jar reads: **Ethanol**
The note in the man's hand reads: **Request for an ethanol allotment**

B. Ivanov, 1963
425 x 566 mm

[Alcohol is] not sold to those wearing uniforms!

Evidently, this lady doesn't care
who buys cigarettes and wine.
Though he's just a kid,
he's not *her* son – but someone else's.

E. Osipov, c.1985
330 x 440 mm

КОГДА СЮДА
ИДЕТ ЗАРПЛАТА,
ТО НЕМИНУЕМА
РАСПЛАТА.

When the week's pay goes in here,
The day of reckoning is near.

E. Abezgus, 1965
913 x 574 mm

Drunkenness – corrupts.

U. Galkus. Lithuanian SSR, 1984
878 x 564 mm

Drunkenness won't be tolerated!

H. H. Papirnaya, V. A. Radko, Y. I. Sherstobitov, 1986
610 x 414 mm

A drunk behind the wheel is a criminal!

H. H. Papirnaya, V. A. Radko, Y. I. Sherstobitov, 1986
610 x 414 mm

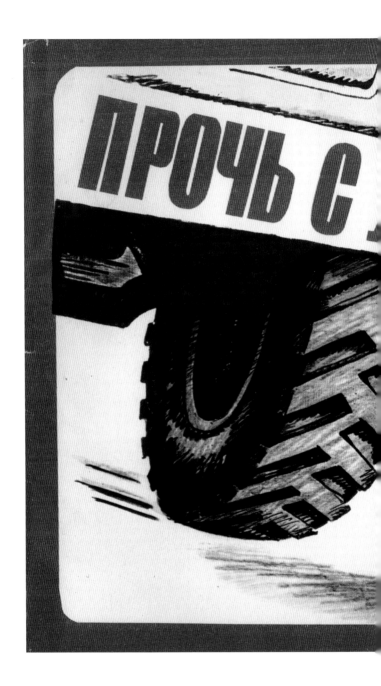

Out of my way!

Художник В. ЖЕЛОБИНСКИЙ
Стихи В. ХОЧИНСКОГО

РОГИ!

ПОДБОРКА
ПЛАКАТОВ

V. Zhelobinsky, 1987
Booklet cover, 210 x 280 mm

Say no to drinking.

Artist unknown, c.1986
440 x 270 mm

**A drunken driver
is a criminal.**

Artist unknown, c.1986
525 x 440 mm

No to drinking!

Artist unknown, c.1988
650 x 480 mm

A drunk behind the wheel is a criminal.

V. F. Bahin, Ukrainian SSR, 1985
440 x 285 mm

Drinking alcohol will cripple you for life!

Artist unknown, 1981
600 x 404 mm

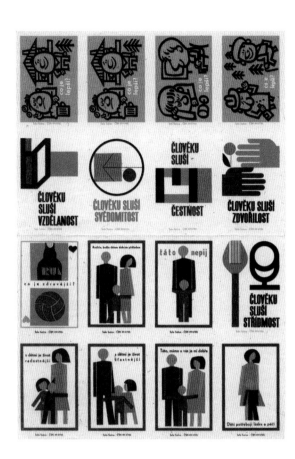

Which is better?

Education befits a man.
Conscientiousness befits a man.
Honesty befits a man.
Courtesy befits a man.

Which is healthier?
Parents, be a good example to your children.
Daddy, don't drink.
Moderation befits a man.

With children life is so much happier.
With children life is so much happier.
Dad, Mum, I'm happy with you.
Children need kindness and care.

Artist unknown, Czechoslovakia, c.1986
Matchbox label sheet, 180 x 145 mm

The alphabet of health.

Text in the squares with arrows reads: **Theatre, Museum, Playing Field, Cinema, Park, Tours**

I am for a healthy lifestyle!

L. Klevitsky, 1988
550 x 430 mm

Three's a crowd.

There's no doubt, in anyone's mind:
There's no place for spirits in love!

Text on the bottle reads: **Port**

B. Semenov, 1988
440 x 330 mm

ФАКТ НА ЛИЦЕ

Spiritus vini means 'alcohol' in Latin.
Drunkards have always loved it.
If you take a liking to it at work,
You'll turn into a vessel in no time.

Facing the truth.

D. Oboznenko, c.1986
440 x 330 mm

Потеря минуты
нам дорого стоит—

ДОЛОЙ
ОПОЗДАНИЯ,
ПРОГУЛЫ,
ПРОСТОИ!

Time wasted has a high price –
Down with showing up late, skipping work, and procrastinating!

M. Abramov, 1980s
440 x 330 mm

ВИНО
СКОТИНИТ
И ЗВЕРИТ
ЧЕЛОВЕКА...
Ф. М. Достоевский

'Wine coarsens and brutalises a man.'
Fyodor Dostoyevsky

L. Pomyansky, 1988
650 x 480 mm

He treated himself to some booze,
And ruined his good name.

He rushed to the grocery shop, swift as the wind,
Still firm on both his feet.

Then he called up some buddies,
And they formed 'three of a kind'.*

After the 'meeting' adjourned,
He headed home on all fours.

He'll end up in a drunk tank,
With a bill for one.

* The notion of being one 'third' of a 'three of a kind' comes from the idea of splitting the cost (of alcohol) three ways. Until 1971 the price of a 0.5 litre bottle of Moskovskaya vodka was 2.87 rubles. In 1958, Khrushchev initiated a decree that prohibited serving vodka in cheap public catering facilities. Those who were used to having a shot on their way home from work were now forced to buy a whole bottle. To cut the cost, it would be split three ways – usually with two complete strangers. The initiator would stand outside a shop surreptitiously signalling potential drinking partners by placing three fingers on his lapel or outside his pocket, often tapping them on the fabric.

N. Muratov, 1985
440 x 330 mm

В ПОДВОРОТНЕ УГОСТИЛСЯ — С ДОБРЫМ ИМЕНЕМ ПРОСТИЛСЯ.

Мчался в «Гастроном», как ветер лих,
На своих, как говорится, на двоих.

А потом собрал дружков своих,
И сообразили на троих.

После «теплой» встречи выпивох
Он домой побрел на четырех.

Вытрезвитель ждет теперь его —
Счет получит там на одного.

Художник Н. ИГНАТОВ
Стихи С. СМИРНОВСКОГО

Will you be the third?*

* See page 114.

O. Karpenko, Ukrainian SSR, 1988
900 x 580 mm

Want to be the third?*

Text on the bottle reads: **Vodka**

* See page 114.

E. Kazhdan, 1985
440 x 330 mm

Bottle in the coffin reads:
Fruit-and-berry wine
Bottles at sides read: **Juice**
part of the word **Golden**
(a brand of a carbonated
soft drink popular in
the USSR)

**Gradually, juices and soft
drinks will push vodka out
of the market.**

V. Boldirev, 1986
pages 118–123:
Screen printed poster set
550 x 350 mm

**There is but one step
from wine to guilt.
Alcoholism is our
society's enemy!**

D. Palui, 1987

Alcoholism maims you. Alcoholics are morally crippled!

The number of stars represents the grade markings on a bottle of cognac –
five stars meaning five or more years.

V. Chausov, 1987

**Drinking – Out!
Sobriety is the law!**

V. Boldirev, 1986

**He made bootlegged
vodka to sell. He was
caught red-handed
and taken into custody.**

A. Tanel, 1986

**When a worker is sozzled,
His productivity equals zero!**

Text in the brickwork reads: **Flaw**

A. Gerasimov, 1986

Drinking and hooliganism go hand in hand!

Text on the club reads: **Vodka**

V. Miroshnikov, 1987

He's prepared to drink anything to get high –
And that is the bottom line!

Text on the aerosol can reads: **Prima** [a brand of insecticide]

V. I. Dorohov, 1987

It might just cave in!

This is not a picnic!

Interred...

Wreath ribbon reads: **Bonuses,
Benefits, Paid Trip, Housing Voucher**

Alcohol destroys families

pages 124–127:
K. Ivanov, 1988
Postcard set, 210 x 150 mm

ПЬЯНСТВУ— БОЙ!

Drunkenness won't be tolerated!

Wine goes in, brains go out.

Injury accompanies alcoholism!

Drinking parents are enemies
of their own progeny!

On the knot: **People's unanimity
U**proots the evil!

Two ways of crossing the finish line.

Down with moonshine!

Use it before it's too late!

Lifebuoy text reads: **Narcologist***

* In English, 'narcologist' denotes someone who studies drug abuse and addiction. Here it means a doctor specialising in treatment of (alcohol) addiction.

Not a drop of alcohol for children!

Text bottom right reads: '**Took a shot, then took another...**'*

* A phrase from a well-known rhyme.

НЕ ПОДХОДИ!

Художник В. ЖАРИНОВ

Stay away!

V. Zharinov, 1977
480 x 325 mm

We will stop alcoholism.

V. Arseenkov, 1986
550 x 430 mm

A 'Pro' Drunk.

**Why is he hovering by the lathe so timidly for hours on end?
The reason is the cork, and the 40 degrees inside.**

Text on the overalls reads: **Vodka 40°**

Kukryniksy*, c.1972
660 x 480 mm

* The collective name derived from the combined names of the satrical cartoonists, Mikhail Kupriyanov, Porfiri Krylov and Nikolai Sokolov, who became famous for their caricatures of Fascist leaders during WWII.

Failing to report to work is a form of labour desertion.

N. Sviridov, 1988
653 x 480 mm

A team method is simple yet effective. Applying it we'll squeeze all drunks out!

Text on the sleeve reads: **(Worker's) Team**

M. Abromov and A. Andreev, 1983
430 x 270 mm

Drunkenness won't be tolerated!

V. Zharinov, 1977
525 x 405 mm

**Remember, kids:
the [wine] glass is
responsible for
many evils.**

A. G. Rudkovich, 1983
600 x 465 mm

**Studying is your job.
Wine is not a friend
of that job.**

A. G. Rudkovich, 1983
600 x 465 mm

Want to be healthy and nimble?
Follow our advice – don't even taste wine.

A. G. Rudkovich, 1983
600 x 465 mm

A visual aid for designers and organisers of visual propaganda.
Number 2

The Komsomol Searchlight
The Perestroika Policy
Socialist Responsibilities

The Lightning
Our News

The Perestroika Policy
Attention: Advanced Experience

Advanced Experience for the Production Process
Self-Management. Acceleration

Bring Science to the Production Process

Save/Preserve Our Resources

Congratulations
Thank you for your labour
Wishes of happiness
An apartment for each family

Sobriety is the norm
A note for the shirker

V. Trubanov, 1989
970 x 668 mm

Milk
Alcohol

Artist unknown, Peoples Republic of Bulgaria, c.1986
Matchbox label, 50 x 35 mm

right:
Don't get children accustomed to alcohol.
This is a crime.

E. L. Kudryashov, Ukrainian SSR, 1985
440 x 290 mm

НЕ ПРИВЧАЙТЕ
ДІТЕЙ
ДО АЛКОГОЛЮ

ЦЕ ЗЛОЧИН

Alcohol

Artist unknown, c.1985
650 x 480 mm

**Stop –
before it's too late.**

Artist unknown, c.1985
650 x 480 mm

Cause – alcoholism!

E. Tsvik, 1985
650 x 480 mm

Don't be enslaved to the bad habit.

Artist unknown, c.1985
650 x 480 mm

Snake body: **Alcoholism**

E. Bor, 1985
650 x 480 mm

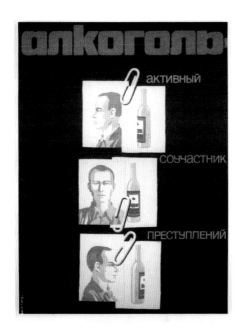

Alcohol is an active accomplice in crime.

Artist unknown, c.1985
650 x 480 mm

To health!

Artist unknown, c.1985
650 x 480 mm

The profiteer is our worst enemy.

Artist unknown, c.1985
650 x 480 mm

Downed one glass, then another...*

* A line from a popular folk rhyme.

Artist unknown, c.1985
650 x 480 mm

A rich inner content.

Artist unknown, c.1985
650 x 480 mm

Vodka brings along: Crime, **H**ooliganism, **S**hoddy workmanship,
Licentiousness, **P**arasitism, **A**bsenteeism

Text on the bottle reads: **Alcoholism**

E. Bor, 1985
650 x 480 mm

**We will overcome!
Alcoholism.**

E. Bor, 1985
650 x 480 mm

**Alcohol is the enemy
of production.**

Artist unknown, c.1985
650 x 480 mm

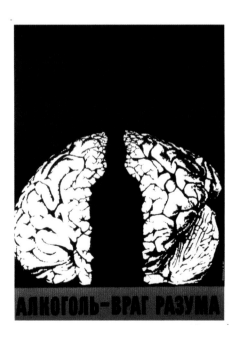

**Alcohol is the enemy
of reason.**

V. Sinukaev, 1985
650 x 480 mm

'General words on the deteriorating effects of drinking'
This is not uncommon...

E. Bor, 1985
650 x 480 mm

С МОЛОКОМ МАТЕРИ

Страшное соседство—
Алкоголь и детство.

With the mother's milk.
Alcohol and childhood is a terrifying mix.

V. Travin, 1980s
440 x 330 mm

Ruining your health, family, and progeny.

Artist unknown, 1980s
650 x 480 mm

The future of children.

V. Zundalev, 1985
550 x 430 mm

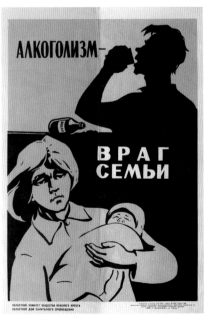

Alcoholism destroys families.

Artist unknown, 1976
480 x 375 mm

An exchange.

Text on the blanket reads: **Resolution of the People's Court of Termination of Parental Rights**

Artist unknown, 1980s
650 x 480 mm

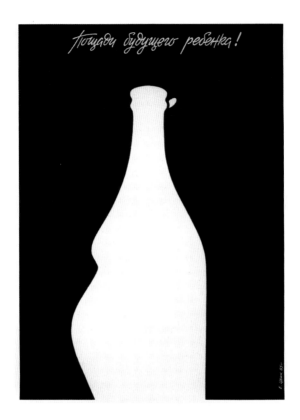

Пощади будущего ребенка!

Spare the future child!

E. Tsvik, 1985
650 x 480 mm

overleaf:
The child of love... of alcohol.

They are prepared to give away anything for vodka.
They don't care that their child will suffer for it.

B. Semenov, 1988
330 x 430 mm

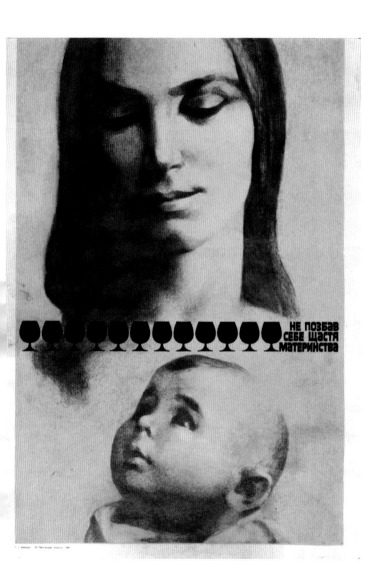

Do not deprive yourself of the happiness of motherhood.

G. I. Shevtsov, Ukrainian SSR, 1988
440 x 290 mm

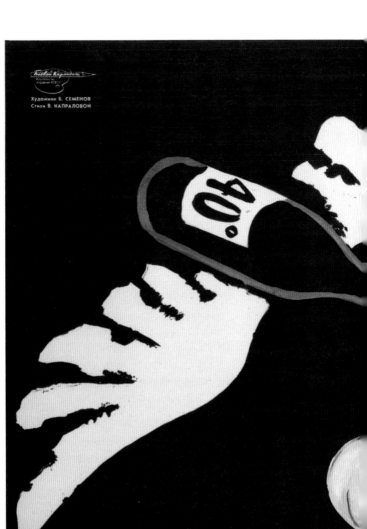

Художник Б. СЕМЕНОВ
Стихи В. КАПРАЛОВОЙ

ДИТЯ ЛЮБВИ... К СПИРТНОМУ

За водочку готовы все отдать,
Плевать, что их ребенку век страдать...

И СМЕХ, И ГРЕХ
подборка плакатов «Боевого карандаша»
Издательство «Художник РСФСР»
Изогнабинат «Художник РСФСР»

Drunkenness is not
your friend,
Your friend is a tree.
It cures any ailment.

D. Palui, 1987

pages 160–165:
Screen printed poster set
550 x 350 mm

The light of such lanterns
will go out,
If we say no to them
all together.

R. Shutenko, 1987

Limited in legal capacity.

Since an alcoholic is capable of drinking away everything,
Having disregarded the rights of his family and society,
The court strips him of a number of rights,
By rendering him 'limited in legal capacity'.

E. Kurmanaevskaya, 1987

'The main objective of community courts is to prevent infringements of the law, educate citizens by persuasion and social pressure, create the environment of intolerance of non-compliance with work discipline and any anti-social behaviour.'
A community court is harsh and just, because a collective stands behind it.

Text on the waste container reads: **Rejects**

S. Nesterov, 1987

Out of my way, glass of booze,
Out of my way, intoxicating poison.
May true revelry burn hot and bright
In my chest!

A. Kurmanaevsky, 1987

**Behind a nonalcoholic
façade is a disgusting scene.**

A. Mardirosov, 1987

**Everywhere and at all times,
A drunk behind the wheel
will lead to a disaster.**

A. Ksenita, 1986

Stay ahead,
Don't drag behind.
Fight alcoholism,
Fight for sobriety!

Text on the broken bottle reads: **Crime, Alcoholism, Shoddy Work,**
Absenteeism, Divorce, Injuries
Text on the hammer reads: **Decree**

A. Tanel, 1987

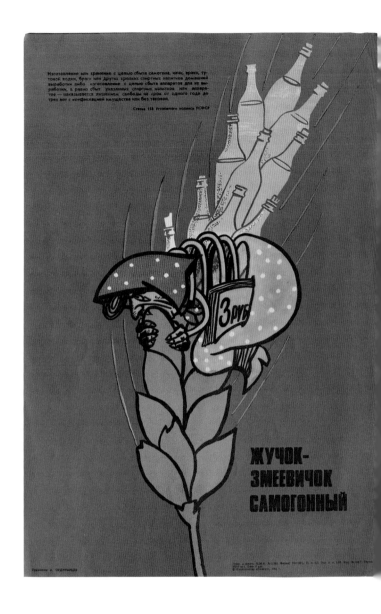

Coil-Pipe Moonshine Beetle.

Notes in the beetle's pocket read: **3 rubles**

A. Ordinartsev, 1981
480 x 320 mm

Alcohol is a cause for injuries.

D. Brodskii and V. Suglobov, 1987

610 x 414 mm

No Admittance!
At any plant or factory, we declare war on drinking!

B. Ivanov, 1980s
440 x 330 mm

The man on telephone declares: **'We punish for drinking, regardless of rank or position!'**
Sign above the door reads: **Anti-Alcohol Committee.**
Don't try to cover up a drunkard, it will turn out badly for you.

E. Osipov, 1985
440 x 330 mm

СТОЛОНАЧАЛЬНИК

Верим, кончится раздолье
Пьянкам с болью в голове...
Славься, трезвое застолье
С самоваром во главе!

A Table Superior.

We believe that one day will end,
Drunken parties followed by hangover...
Long live nonalcoholic table gatherings,
With a samovar towering over!

N. Bayev, 1985
440 x 330 mm

'We'll finish it all after lunch.'

D. Oboznenko, 1985
330 x 440 mm

overleaf:
At a crossroads...

**We see three roads here,
All leading to disaster.
To find the 'safe way',
Forget about vodka.**

Text on the bottle reads: **Vodka**

N. Bayev, 1985
330 x 440 mm

„ЛИЧНОЕ КЛЕЙМО"

С ним всегда бывает так:
Как напьётся — гонит брак.
Нам пора для пользы дела
Гнать пьянчугу-бракодела.

A personal stamp.

It's always the same with him:
Once he gets drunk, he produces faulty goods.
It will only be for everyone's good,
If we kick the bungler out.

Text on the bottle-stamp and bungled sprocket wheels reads: **Rejects**

V. Zhelobinsky, 1985
440 x 330 mm

Художник Н. БАЕВ
Стихи Д. ТОЛМАЧЕВА

ПРИВЛЕКАЮТСЯ К ОТВЕТСТВЕННОСТИ
Подборка плакатов «Боевого карандаша»
Издательство «Художник РСФСР»
Изготовляет «Художник РСФСР»

Три пути л
К бедам в
Чтоб найти
Водку, пья

ть,

Text inside the speech bubble reads: **I'm with my better 'half' and a 'little one'.***

**The aficionado of alcohol,
Has loaded himself.
He's eager to get to a resort,
But will end up in a drunk tank.**

* A 'half' refers to a 0.5 litre bottle of vodka, 'little one' is a 0.25 litre.

L. Kaminsky, 1985
440 x 330 mm

Will be brought to trial.

D. Oboznenko, 1985
440 x 330 mm

The sign above the salesgirl's reads: **NON Wine Section***

On the salesgirl's mouth: **a ten rouble note** (c.1961)

On the counter only juices – just as the law dictates.
But one can plainly see what brings the most profit.

* The 'non' prefix turns the adjective *vinny* ('wine') into *nevinny* ('innocent').

V. Zavyalov, 1985
440 x 330 mm

'Catering van'.

Opening hours: 7 PM to 2 PM.
No lunch break.

He used to be a driver.
Now he's a profiteer.

G. Kovenchuk, 1985
440 x 330 mm

'Talents' and 'admirers'.*

Bootleggers apply
The advances of technological progress in practice:

And the wicked poison slowly
Flows, like in the olden days, for profit.

* After the play of the same name by Alexander Ostrovsky.

Y. Trunev, 1985
330 x 440 mm

He quit.

The pages of the calendar are vodka labels, each with a day of the week written on it.

He tortured his organism day after day,
And quit only when his final day arrived.

E. Osipov, 1988
440 x 330 mm

No, we didn't reap or plough,
We just had a picnic in the field.
As for the bread itself, Zina and I think
There's plenty of it in the shop.

J. Efimovsky, 1985
330 x 440 mm

On 'sick leave'.

You don't really need a note from your doctor
To take a dose of Stolichnaya.

V. Kyunnap, 1985
330 x 440 mm

Художник В. ЖЕЛОБИНСКИЙ
Стихи А. ШКЛЯРИНСКОГО

Местный мастер
　　　　берет «по таксе».

Сколько!
　　　Видно по этой таксе.

— ИЩИ МАСТЕРА !

The local plumber charges 'according to the price list'.
How much exactly you can judge from this 'dog'.

'Find the plumber!'

V. Zhelobinsky, 1985
330 x 440 mm

БУДЬ МУЖЧИНОЙ!

Родители сынку твердят: «Хлебни!»
Одну всего лишь рюмочку, а ну-ка!
Хлебнут же горя горького они,
Коль впрок пойдет сыночку их наука.

Be a man!

The parents tell their son, 'Take a gulp.
Just a small glass, come on!'
They'll take a gulp of bitterness,
If the son takes their lesson to heart.

J. Efimovsky, 1985
330 x 440 mm

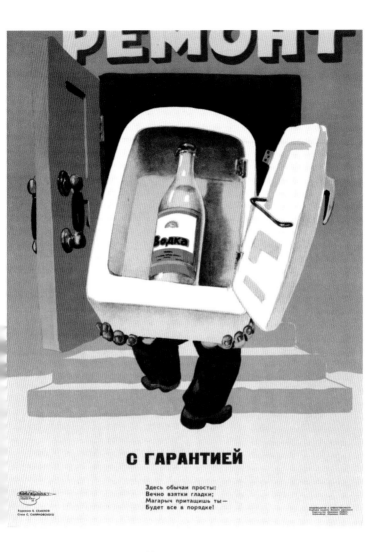

Above the entrance: **Repair Shop**

Comes with a warranty.

The custom is really simple here:
No accountability.
If you want to have things done,
You've got to bribe them with some booze.

V. Semenov, 1985
330 x 440 mm

This is a crime.

V. Feklyaev, 1986
440 x 290 mm

The ruining of hope.

S. Alekseev, 1986
440 x 290 mm

Ministry of Health Warning:
Cologne is unsafe for consumption.

Artist unknown, c.1985
Newspaper cartoon, 120 x 120 mm

ТАК ВОТ ГДЕ ТАИЛАСЬ ПОГИБЕЛЬ МОЯ

'So this is where I find my demise.'*

* A quote from Alexander Pushkin's poem 'The Ballad of Oleg the Wise'.

Artist unknown, c.1986
380 x 525 mm

Hold it right there!

Text above the window reads: **Pay window**
Text underneath on a piece of paper reads: **Bonus**
Text on the red sleeve reads: **People's Inspection**

V. Elistratov, K. Solomyannii, M. Ushats, 1986
Magazine cartoon, 160 x 120 mm

Простая арифметика

Simple arithmetic.

Text on the bottle reads: **Vodka**
Text on the faulty part reads: **Rejects**

V. Elistratov, K. Solomyannii, M. Ushats, 1986
Magazine cartoon, 80 x 200 mm

Пьянству — нет!

Say no to drinking!

Text on the sheet of paper reads: **Health and recreation programme**

V. Elistratov, K. Solomyannii, M. Ushats, 1986
Magazine cartoon, 160 x 140 mm

In the hands of a 'master'.

P. D. Yegorov,
Ukrainian SSR, 1987
440 x 280 mm

A sponger's travails.

P. D. Yegorov,
Ukrainian SSR, 1987
440 x 280 mm

A dangerous mentor!

P. D. Yegorov, Ukrainian SSR, 1987
440 x 280 mm

Shame on them!

P. D. Yegorov, Ukrainian SSR, 1987
440 x 280 mm

His inner world.

P. D. Yegorov, Ukrainian SSR, 1987
440 x 280 mm

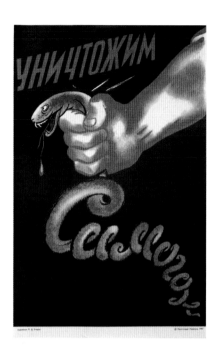

We'll eradicate bootlegging.

P. D. Yegorov,
Ukrainian SSR, 1987
440 x 280 mm

Scram!

P. D. Yegorov,
Ukrainian SSR, 1987
440 x 280 mm

Recommendation: An excellent employee, full of initiatives, creative, voluntary group activist.

That'll do.

P. D. Yegorov, Ukrainian SSR, 1987
440 x 280 mm

ПРОГУЛЫ, ПЬЯНСТВО, БРАК

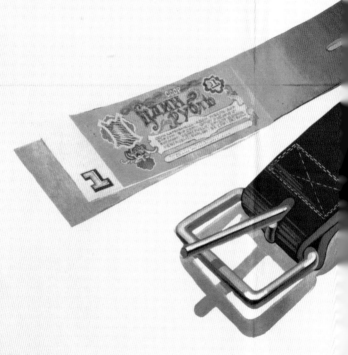

Художник Ю. БЛИНОВ
Редактор Р. Энгель. Худож. редактор Ю. Иванов
Техн. редактор Л. Никитина
© Издательство «Плакат». Москва. 1986 г.
Подп. в печать 11.06.87. А-12940. Формат 70×100 1/8. П. л. 5,0. Усл. п. л. 0,80. Усл. кр.-отт. 2,6. Изд.
№ 10-091329. Тираж 50 000 экз. Цена 9 коп. Печать офсетная. Бумага офсетная. Заказ 1238. Типография
издательства «Плакат». г. Тула, ул. Ф. Энгельса, 150

к 5020109860-535. КЭ-44-13-81
 085(01)-84

Absenteeism,
Drinking,
Shoddy workmanship.   We won't tolerate this!

НЕ ПОТЕРПИМ!

Y. Vlinov, 1988
480 x 646 mm

It is parents who drink,
It is their children who have to pay for it.

I. M. Maisgrovsky, 1986
420 x 140 mm

7. You're drinking away your money!

pages 199–201:
Artist unknown, c.1986
Set of factory posters, 290 x 230 mm

16. Imprisonment for up to one year.

17. From drinking buddies.

The leaves of the wreath are labels of various alcoholic drinks.

20. Untangle yourself, before it's too late...

25. Alcohol is responsible for injuries.

СКОЛЬКО ВОДКИ – СТОЛЬКО СЛЁЗ
ТЫ СЕМЬЕ СВОЕЙ ПРИНЁС!

ПЬЯНИЦ – К ОТВЕТУ!

ПРЕМИЯ.
ЛЬГОТНАЯ
ПУТЁВКА
В ДОМ
ОТДЫХА.
ОЧЕРЁДНОСТЬ
НА
ЖИЛПЛОЩАДЬ.

продажа
водки
в районе
производствен-
ных предприятий
запрещена

26. Call drunks to account!

The crossed-out list behind the
drunken worker reads: **Bonus,
Sanatorium voucher,
Flat allotment.***

* The Soviet system allotted free flats
to those who were eligible. The
applicant was put in a queue,
and the wait period could often last for
many years.

**30. You have brought as much tears
to your family as the vodka you
have drunk.**

**23. The sale of vodka in the vicinity
of production facilities is
prohibited.**

The image is an amended version of the
famous painting *A Knight at the Crossroads*
(1878) by Viktor Vasnetsov.

Alcohol paves the way to decay.

Drinking may result in a crime.

pages 202–203:
Artist unknown, Hungarian Red Cross, 1960s
Matchbox labels, 50 x 35 mm

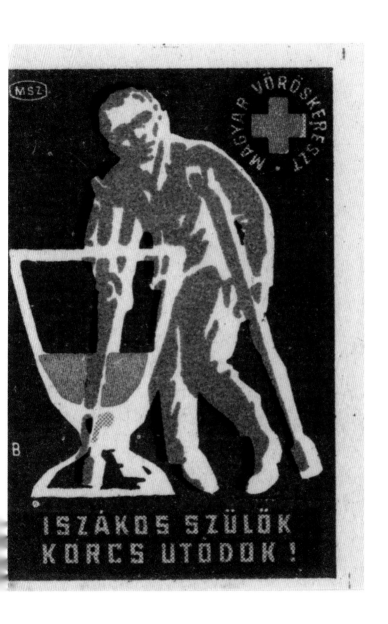

Drinking parents bring degenerate progeny!

**If you can't beat it yourself,
Seek medial advice.**

Text in the red cross reads: **Alcoholism is treatable**

V. L. Kondratev, 1970
442 x 563 mm

Если в бригаде—подобные дяди,
С планом приходится туго бригаде.

Художник О. МАСЛЯКОВ
Стихи М. ВЛАДИМОВА и М. РАСКАТОВА

Text on the arrow reads: **Meeting the target**
Text on the jar reads: **Pickles**

If there are men like this in a brigade,
It will have a hard time meeting its target.

O. Maslyakov, c.1986
525 x 440 mm

Moving through the mundane life of petty bourgeoise cliques, with exaggerated disgust, we will change the face of both personal and public lives.
– Vladimir Mayakovsky

V. Dorohov, 1986
430 x 270 mm

'Out with drunks!'
We'll say out loud.
They only cause debauchery and equipment faults.
– Vladimir Mayakovsky

V. Kozlov, A Reshetov, V. Chernov, 1988
430 x 270 mm

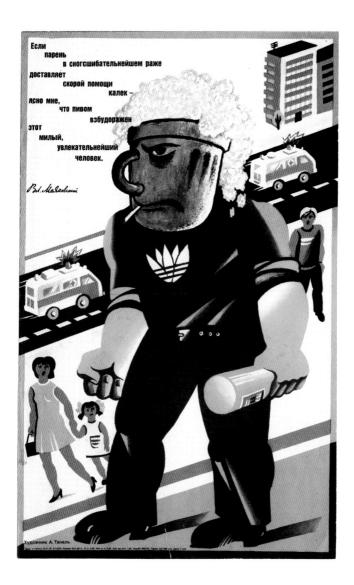

If a man goes on a rampage, and leaves behind
injured people for ambulances to take away,
it is clear to me that the good-natured and
interesting person has been worked up by having
too many beers.

– Vladimir Mayakovsky

A. Tanel, 1986
430 x 270 mm

**Down with drunks!
With drunks like him,
Machinery will rust and stall.**

Text on the bottle reads: **Vodka**

V. Latishev, 1986
pages 208–209:
Poster set, 440 x 285 mm

Text on the clock reads:
Electronika*
Text on the bottle reads: **Vodka**

**Comrade,
keep your eyes peeled,
So that an eight-hour
work shift doesn't turn into
a three-hour one.**

* A brand name used for a variety of
electronic products – from digital
watches and calculators to
computers.

РЕСПУБЛИКА НАША В ОПАСНОСТИ.
В ДВЕРЬ
ЛЕЗЕТ
НЕМЫСЛИМЫЙ ЗВЕРЬ.
МОРДА МАТОВЫМ РЫКОМ ГУЛКА,
ЛАПЫ—
В КУЛАКАХ.
БЕЗМОЗГЛЫЙ,
И ДВЕ НОГИ
ДЛЯ ЛЯГАНИЙ.
ВОТ-ПОРТРЕТ ХУЛИГАНИЙ.

Our Republic is at peril,
A monster is trying to squeeze in the doorway.
A muffled roar comes from his mouth,
His paws adorned with fists.
It is brainless and has two legs for kicking.
This is a portrait of a hooligan.

Sobriety is the norm.

Combatting alcoholism is everybody's personal responsibility.
In this combat nobody should demonstrate indifference. Fighting
for a healthy, alcohol-free lifestyle is fighting for people's health
and happiness.

A. U. Borodchak, 1986
610 x 440 mm

Don't drink your life away.

I. M. Maistrovsky, 1977
570 x 385 mm

This is bad for your health.

V. F. Bahin, Ukrainian SSR, 1987
900 x 585 mm

ТРЕЗВОСТЬ–
НОРМА
ЖИЗНИ

Москва «ПЛАКАТ» 1988

Sobriety is the norm.

Artist unknown, 1988
525 x 405 mm

**I. Urakov
Harming Yourself, Your
Family, and Society**

Book cover, 1978

**V. E. Rozhnov
Alcohol – Enemy of Man**

Booklet cover, 1972
215 x 140 mm

It's not at all difficult to predict
How this 'charming' will end.

On the snake (top to bottom): **Rejects, Skipping work, Injuries**

I. Sychev, 1977
525 x 395 mm

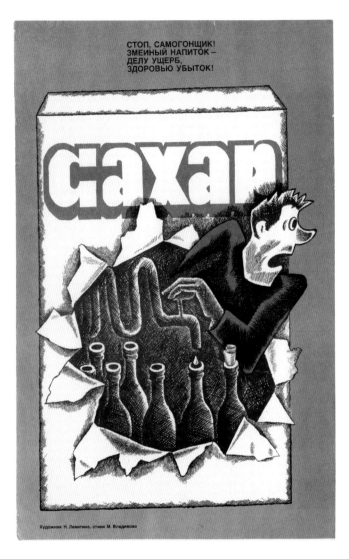

Художник Н. Левитина, стихи М. Владимова

Moonshiner, stop!
Your poison is damaging
To your work,
And your life!

Text on the box reads: **Sugar**

N. Levitina, c.1986
440 x 280 mm

Cause...

and effect...

A. Shchetinin, 1987
670 x 480 mm

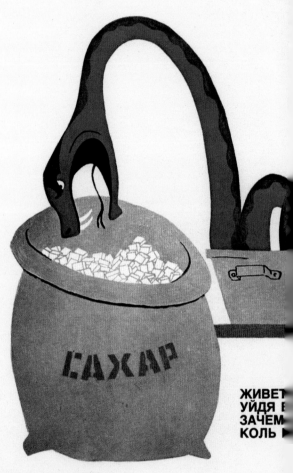

ЖИВЕТ
УЙДЯ I
ЗАЧЕМ
КОЛЬ ►

Художник Е. Гуров, стихи М. Раскатова

He lives, brewing poison,
All 'consumed' by his work...
Why pay him an official salary,
If he already has a means of income?

Text on the bag reads: **Sugar**

E. Gurov, 1987
670 x 480 mm

Warehouse.
A secret padlock...

P. D. Yegorov, Ukrainian SSR, 1987
440 x 280 mm

Increase strict control.

There. Where the absence of control reigns.

P. D. Yegorov, Ukrainian SSR, 1987
440 x 280 mm

Rejects*

* A pun on the alternative meaning of the word *brak* – 'marriage'.

P. D. Yegorov,
Ukrainian SSR, 1987
440 x 280 mm

This is a crime!

A. Braz, 1983
420 x 280 mm

Decree on Increasing the Measures against Drinking.

P. D. Yegorov,
Ukrainian SSR, 1987
440 x 280 mm

Handwriting reads:
'Fire Mr. Myshkin for drinking'.

Text underneath reads:
'Look who's talking?'

P. D. Yegorov,
Ukrainian SSR, 1987
440 x 280 mm

Vodka has brought
Much evil and wrongdoing to the family.

Text on the bottle reads: **Vodka**

I. Fridman, 1977
525 x 400 mm

Come to your senses before it's too late!

A. G. Velichko, 1985
840 x 600 mm

Strong bonds.

Whether a regular or 'special' vodka,
He drowns his sorrows in it anyway.
Once he attaches himself to a bottle,
There's no way you can prise him off.

Kukryniksy (see page 130), 1959
570 x 410 mm

ЦЕНА РЮМКИ

The price of glasses of wine.

Items in the glass clockwise from top left: **Wages**; **Permit for the sanitorium resort 'South'**; **Voucher for a flat**

Artist unknown, c.1978
870 x 560 mm

Этот дядя на селе
Ползимы навеселе!

This village man,
Is drunk for half of winter!

Text on the bottle labels reads: **Mon.**, **Tue.**, **Wed.**, **Thur.**, **Fri.**, **Sat.**, **Sun.**

Художник В. ЖАРИНОВ
Стихи М. РАСКАТОВА

V. Zharinov, 1977
395 x 525 mm

The Origins and Significance of Alcoholism in Russia

ПИТЬЕВОЙ
drinking

What and How Russians Drink

Alexei Plutser-Sarno

ОПРЕДЕЛЯТЬ determines

'Russians, more than any other people in the world, are devoted to drinking. After overindulging in spirits, like savage beasts they fall without measure or restraint on whatever undertaking their passionate desires lead them to. The sin of drinking is equally widespread across all estates – men and women, young and old, ecclesiastics and laity, commoners and nobility – to such a degree that the sight of a drunkard lying in a puddle on the street is an everyday occurrence.'

The above account is taken from *Travels of the Ambassadors sent by Frederic, Duke of Holstein, to the Great Duke of Muscovy and the King of Persia* (1647, with many subsequent expanded editions) by the German traveller Adam Olearius. Having visited Russia four times in the decade from 1634, Olearius was familiar with both its language and its traditions.

* A paraphrase from Karl Marx's book *A Contribution to the Critique of Political Economy* (1859); 'The mode of production of material life conditions the general process of social, political and intellectual life. It is not the consciousness of men that determines their existence, but their social existence that determines their consciousness.'

consciousness*

сознание

The amount of alcohol Russians consumed may have seemed staggering and the methods of consumption astonishing, but historical descriptions by foreign travellers are often inaccurate. Prohibited from moving around freely, foreigners were able to visit only large towns, and even then required special permission from the czar. As a result, their stories of debauchery relate to drinking-houses in cities at a time when more than 90% of the population lived in the countryside. These were peasants, who drank in moderation: their lives followed a cyclical, measured trajectory that made alcoholism a rare exception. Peasants drank mostly kvass, braga and mead; vodka in this period was only 20% alcohol and very expensive. It was a drink of the elite, given by the czar to members of his retinue as a special favour.

Over the next four hundred years, however, conditions changed, with the authorities promoting heavy drinking among the populace, to their exclusive financial advantage. By the 19th century the situation had become catastrophic. With the establishment of an industrial society and the formation of the working class, a great number of people were separated from their peasant communes, which had regulated alcohol consumption. In the 20th century both the nobility and peasantry were eradicated as classes, and alcoholism became a large-scale phenomenon among the lumpenproletariat. Vodka and samogon (moonshine) were now the drinks of choice, yet habits of consumption remained the same: people would gulp down entire glasses or even bottles of spirits all in one go, often without even a chaser. This popular joke reflects typical Russian measures of alcohol:

A man goes to the doctor complaining about his health.

'Do you drink or smoke?' the doctor asks.

'I drink, but only in moderation,' says the man.

'And what exactly do you mean by "moderation"?'

'Well, no more than a litre of vodka, but not in one go! I spread it out it over the course of the day.'

Drinking to the end of the bottle

Russians drink lots, quickly, in what could be described as a heroic fashion. At the start of Venedikt Yerofeyev's prose-poem *Moscow-Petushki* ('Moscow to the End of the Line', 1969–70) the protagonist downs 800ml of vodka, a bottle of wine, a litre of beer and finally 'something else that cost me six rubles'. In 1970 six rubles would have bought another bottle of vodka and two more bottles of wine. For a drinking man in Russia, consuming two and a half bottles of vodka, two bottles of wine, and one or two litres of beer over the course of a day (including late into the night) would seem a realistic, albeit maximum, amount. Having downed it all, the protagonist falls into a state of unconsciousness.

Drinkers who can consume large quantities of alcohol are respected by their peers. There are many jokes about the 'sport' of 'litreball', in which the Russian 'athlete' always beats his British, American or French counterparts: 'The French athlete is in the ring now. He drinks ten ladles of vodka and… And he breaks down. It's all over for the French athlete. Now the British contestant enters the ring. He downs twenty ladles of vodka and… And he too breaks down. Now it's the Russian athlete's turn in the ring. He downs ten ladles… twenty… thirty… And… he breaks… He breaks the handle of the ladle!'

Drinking 'all in one go' is a centuries-old marker of decent behaviour: 'The prince… usually drinks his cup bottoms up and then encourages others to follow suit', as Olearius observed. So at a party, or even when drinking alone, every shot must be consumed in its entirety, 'to the end', and the bottle too must be 'killed'. Eating and drinking are sacred so it is seen as a sin to leave food on your plate or vodka in the bottle. The leading principle here is 'Sufficient unto the day is the evil thereof' (meaning, 'live in the present, without a care for tomorrow'). Not finishing your shot of vodka after a toast denotes disrespect to the person giving the toast and runs the risk that the wish within it will not be fulfilled. The lyrics of singer-songwriter Vladimir Vysotsky (1938–1980) poignantly evoke the need to drink until the bottle (or purse) is empty:

'I drank my money
All of it…
I earned it and I spent it all on drinks,
And I'll do it again, and again…'

As far back as the 19th century an abstainer would be seen as a weak, spineless creature: 'Refusing to drink was tantamount to abasing yourself,' Mikhail Zabylin reported in his encyclopedic *Russian People* (1880). When drinking alone the usual dose is between 100ml and 200ml; in (male) company a bottle of vodka is shared equally and in its entirety.

Russians' attitudes to their own drinking habits are both blithe and fatalistic, epitomised by the saying: 'If you don't drink or smoke, you'll die healthy.' A common cry after downing the first glass is, 'No delay between the first and the second' – followed promptly by another round. Official statistics show that every year thousands of Russians die from alcohol-related problems without even counting those who die without a precise medical diagnosis or who render themselves permanently disabled through drink. To foreigners, drinking in Russia resembles an intricate method of suicide, a feat of self-destruction.

Often drinking takes place without the mitigating effects of chasers or food. The drinker's motto is: 'Snacks and chasers don't expand your mind, but only weaken the drink's strength.' This suggests a view of food as sinful (gluttony) while vodka is treated with reverence as a magic potion, an attitude that dates back to the Middle Ages. To quote Zabylin: 'O Lord Drunkenness, Wild Head! Crawl not with your head down, crawl up to the sun. I know thee not, where you live. Up the soggy tree, crawl up to your master… Lord Drunkenness shall reign like a czar in his domain.'

While the expression 'drinking dry' implies the rejection of chasers or food to accompany a drink, there is an ongoing tradition of following your drink with a 'sniff' – where the drinker raises a ball of rye bread, an onion, the sleeve of a garment or just the back of the hand to his nose and inhales. This custom is reflected in the language, with expressions such as 'drinking with fabric', 'with a fist' or 'with the nose'.

Binge drinking

The habit of drinking for days at a time is a sad reality of life in Russia. What counts as a binge can be defined by the duration of the session, which must involve the steady consumption of large quantities of spirits over a period of between three days (minimum) and several months. Someone who drinks for a day or two is not considered to be on a binge (this is reflected in such sayings as 'day one is drinking; day two is the hair of the dog' or 'two days is not a binge, it's an extended party'). A binge drinker is inebriated early in the morning: someone who drinks on a regular basis but not every day is viewed not as an alcoholic but as a boozer, while consumption of alcohol no more than once a day is not considered to be binge drinking. Similarly, people drinking for long periods because of a specific reason (grief, for example) are not thought of as bingers: while it might be noted that the person had been drinking for a month or two, it would be considered legitimate. The 312 days described by Yerofeyev is a comical but realistic timeframe and only someone who had been drinking constantly for over a year would be regarded as a chronic alcoholic.

It is commonly believed that the higher a person's status, the more he should be capable of drinking. Stories of prodigious drinking (and sexual) feats are often associated with the famous, whether the obscene 18th-century poet Ivan Barkov or Peter the Great (1672–1725). Literary talent in particular is linked to a capacity for heavy drinking. As cultural historian Mikhail Epstein wrote in his 1999 essay on Venedikt Yerofeyev: 'In all his competitions with other experienced drunks, he emerged as a victor. When they lay under the table in a sorry state, his eyes were as clear as glass.' Indeed, chronic alcoholism is regarded as an occupational hazard for writers.

In Russia a drunk can be revered, holding a mystical status in the eyes of others: 'the ocean is but knee-deep to a drunk', 'God protects the drunk'. It is as if getting drunk brings one closer to the 'divine'. The more difficult it is to keep the liquor down – the more unpleasant the drink – the higher the status accorded to the act of drinking. The greatest feat is therefore to drink disgusting-tasting liquids not intended for consumption: denatured alcohol, colognes and glue are regarded as akin to magic potions, imparting supernatural strength and powers. Paradoxical as it might seem, the consumption of non-codified drinks can be seen as analogous to fasting, a sanctifying act: according to Epstein, drinking for Yerofeyev was a kind of hair-shirt, an act of penance or asceticism. More than just an occupation, such drinking becomes a calling, a form of martyrdom.

These stereotypes resonate in descriptions of drunks finding repose under the open sky in unpredictable and unsuitable locations. The Finnish ethnologist Matthias Castrén, who journeyed extensively through Russia in the 1840s, wrote: 'The entire snowfield around the Temple of Bacchus was covered with fallen heroes and heroines. At night they lay there, semi-covered with snow. A deadly silence reigned here, whereas savage cries could be heard coming from the tavern… When we arrived at the wedding… everybody had already had quite a bit to drink. Many lay senseless outside, their heads, uncovered, buried in snow… Someone was wandering around with a coffee pot looking for his beloved. Having found her, he poured some vodka down her throat.'

Such circumstances give rise to popular colloquial metaphors including 'to sleep by the earthwork', 'to sleep by the fence', 'to sleep under the bridge' and many more. Comedian Mikhail Zhvanetsky (b. 1934) riffs on this stereotypical behaviour: 'Perhaps the one lying in the ditch won't be able to express himself quickly. Well, then, he will express himself gradually, right there into the ditch, where two or three of his colleagues who lie beside him will be able slowly to soak up what he's expressed.'

Quantity and quality

In Russian folklore vodka is a powerful drink: 'vodka is power, sports are the grave'; 'vodka is a vitamin, according to Ho Chi Minh'. Vodka is even seen as a source of life: 'He asked for special vodka; his gaze was that of a man being tortured. Someone put a bottle of vermouth in the palm of his outstretched hand' (Yerofeyev: *Moscow-Petushki*). Vodka is drunk straight from the bottle because the bottle is regarded as a sacred vessel that can tolerate no intermediaries. To pour vodka from such a vessel into a smaller container is to desecrate it. If a dedicated drinker is offered a drink in a glass, he might respond by stating, 'I don't drink…' Then, after a pause, '…from small containers.'

In polite company a typical serving of vodka is between 30ml and 60ml (between a single and a double shot). As novelist, poet and playwright Yuz Aleshkovsky (b. 1929) describes it in *Nikolay Nikolaevich* (1970), drinking a smaller serving could be perceived as 'refined': 'Don't pour a whole lot – cut it down. That way you get zonked in a more civilised manner, plus your headlights [eyes] don't get all crossed.' In male company it is customary to offer servings of at least 100ml (more than three shots). Vysotsky gives a subtle description of this tradition in one of his songs:

> 'Or maybe he had two by a hundred,
> With someone he shouldn't have had to.'

Yerofeyev is more forthright: 'A 150, followed by 200 more, is just unforgivably little.' Drinking a single serving of 300ml in one go earns genuine respect and admiration – those who achieve this are held in the same esteem as national heroes ready to die for an ideal.

The most brutal Russian method of downing vodka is called 'drinking à la bolt'. This involves swirling the vodka in the bottle to form a vortex, then swinging the head back far enough to allow the liquid to flow directly down the oesophagus, eliminating the need to swallow. The name alludes to the movement of the liquid in the bottle, which is like a bolt being screwed into a nut. Another metaphor is 'to play the bugle', referring to the way the bottle is tipped downwards towards the mouth.

Russians enjoy mixing alcoholic beverages in combinations that would quickly render foreigners insensible. Typical mixtures include beer and vodka (known as yorsh, a 'go-devil': a one-horse sled used for logging), champagne and vodka ('Northern Lights'), cognac and vodka ('brown bear'), port and vodka ('rusty nail'), pure alcohol and water ('white death') and even denatured alcohol or varnish with beer ('silver fox'). When Yerofeyev suggested adding foot deodorant, glue and even DDT to the mix he was parodying a national tradition. But it was Yerofeyev himself who invented 'Tears of a Komsomol Girl' (a combination of lavender water, verbena, herbal lotion, nail varnish, mouthwash and lemonade). An amusing oxymoron, the name suggests that even the young women of Komsomol (the All-Union Leninist Young Communist League) – known for being impervious to sentiment and grief – could not help but weep as they drank this concoction.

Another common Russian practice is the consumption of drinks that are incompatible, one after another, to increase the effect of intoxication: 'drinking vodka without beer is like taking a piss without farting'. The usual method is to start with beer, followed by vodka, chased down by beer: vomiting – 'drinking until you puke' – becomes part of the ritual. Among the names for this process are 'feeding the ichtiander'*, 'launching fireworks (on Victory Day)', 'taking a trip to Riga', and so on. The puking may be followed by 'madness': 'Sometimes he barked like a dog after the holidays, but personally, I think it was only natural after the hangover,' as Aleshkovsky describes it.

By far the most popular mixture is yorsh – vodka mixed with beer in a variety of proportions, from 50ml of vodka with 500ml of beer to 250ml of each. It was common for drinkers to smuggle vodka into bars where they would mix it with their beer when the waiters weren't looking. Yorsh can be drunk anywhere: at home, at work, in a park, in a public toilet. There are several kinds. For instance, the 'smash' involves covering the mug of yorsh with the palm of the hand then smashing it against your knee to carbonate it and so increase its intoxicating effect. The 'Rembrandt' (also called 'The Rooks Have Come Back', after the painting by Alexei Savrasov, 1830–1897) involves combining the ingredients in a mug by pouring one of them very slowly down a handkerchief, so they stay separated. If this is achieved perfectly, the result is called 'an original'; if not, then it's 'a copy'. Adding 50ml of vodka to 500ml of beer creates the 'Early Rembrandt'; the reverse (for example, adding 100ml of beer to 200ml of vodka) is called the 'Late Rembrandt'. 'To Drive the Bear into its Lair' involves taking a sip from a mug filled to the brim with beer then replacing the volume of the sipped amount with vodka. This process is repeated until you are left with a mug full of vodka. ('To Drive the Bear out of its Lair' uses the same method but starts with a mug full of vodka instead of beer.) For 'The Diver' a shot of vodka is lowered into a mug of beer so it falls to the bottom without tipping over.

Pure vodka, however, has always been the most respectable alcoholic beverage and undiluted alcohol is the drink of choice for a true man. Its name, 'pure', invokes ideas of holiness, as does 'white' – the general nickname for vodka – which is also applied to any produce without additives or colouring. The term white exists in juxtaposition to the term red, which surprisingly refers to any wine (red, white or rosé). The common attitude towards wine is one of impersonal disrespect, whereas vodka is treated with reverence. This contempt extends to other beverages: cognac is known as 'horse's piss', champagne as 'shampoo', red wine as 'paint' or 'ink', white wine as 'vinegar' and port as 'insecticide' or 'bum wine'. These terms are used liberally by Aleshkovsky: 'At night, some of us used to bury the remains of the port, ink, or beer by an old apple tree. In the morning you'd dig it up and use it as a hair of the dog.'

* Ichtiander ('fish man') is a character in the science-fiction novel *The Amphibian Man* (1928) by Alexander Belyaev. A scientist transplants a set of shark gills into his son to save his life. As a result, the boy has to spend much of his time in water.

It is traditional to give nicknames not only to all the varieties of vodka, but also to the different sizes of bottle. A 100ml bottle is a shkalik: 'They made me a trades-union member and bring me two shkaliks a day. All because my youth was burned with fougasses [an early form of basic land-mine, here used as a nickname for large bottles – see below]' (Yerofeyev: *Moscow-Petushki*).

Merzavchik, a quarter, the baby, chekushka, a little one, or half-a-jar are common nicknames for the 250ml bottle: 'I pulled the tin cap with my teeth, cutting my lip. I also opened a bottle of Zhigulyovskoe with my teeth. God only knows where I got the strength! Everybody's hands were shaking like those of balalaika players in a traditional orchestra. We poor souls partook of the drink from this tiny, cold bottle, the chekushka, each taking a single gulp of remedy. Whoa! Lord be praised! Forgive us, but we were now saved!' (Aleshkovsky).

The big one, jar, bottle, bubble, half-a-litre are all names for the 500ml bottle. Vysotsky uses a lot of these nicknames in his song 'Once Upon a Time in a Big City':

'All is simple at the counter,
Five people and two half-a-litres.
"Hey, miss, what's with the grumpy face?
You can keep the change!"
I turn around and see
This chick dancing in the middle of the room.
All shiny and sparkling,
Like a star!
So I dropped from under my armpits
Two "big ones" and five "babies".'

'In this big house people caroused
For many, many days.
For the first house on Karetny Ryad
Is always open for friends.
Let's hear it for drinking and carousing!
Let's go get more jars and half-jars.'

Larger bottles – 700ml, 750ml, 800ml or 1 litre – are called the bomb, fire extinguisher, fougasse or goose. Vasily Aksyonov uses the nickname 'geese' in his 1975 novel *The Burn*: 'From his hip pockets he produced his three "geese" – three 750ml bottles of Madeira Rosé by the Ramensky Wine and Liquor Factory.' During the Gorbachev era, the standard Western 330ml bottle or can appeared on the shelves. It was known as a cheburashka, after the famous children's character with a bear-like body and large round ears.

Aftermath: the hangover

The Russian custom of spending every last kopek on alcohol, then drinking it to the very last drop, made a hangover an almost everyday experience for many. Perhaps this is why the idea of treating a hangover as an illness has never been contemplated. It is rare to visit a doctor or even resort to medication to alleviate the symptoms. The traditional cure is a hair of the dog: the consumption of any substance that might contain alcohol, usually leading to further drunkenness.

Suffering from a hangover with no hair-of-the-dog available was a frequent occurrence during the Soviet period. A rich and varied system of hangover prevention developed involving the consumption of certain types of food alongside the alcohol. Pickled tomatoes, cucumbers, wild mushrooms, sauerkraut, salted or smoked fish, fried potatoes, fresh tomatoes, black or red caviar, butter, brown bread, lemon, garlic, onions, horseradish (among other foodstuffs) all contain substances that help the body to metabolise large quantities of alcohol.

If a hangover is unavoidable, then drinking the following can mitigate its effects: beer, the brine from pickles or sauerkraut, kvass, kefir, essences of medicinal herbs, mineral water, and so on. Or the following solid foods can be eaten: dishes preserved in aspic, thick salty broths, fish soup or shi (cabbage soup).

Hangovers have been described in Russian literature many times, but perhaps the most elevated account is in Yerofeyev's *Moscow-Petushki*, where the narrator's sufferings are ironically compared to those of Judas Iscariot: 'I have had a seven-day hangover. And if they were to torture me now, I'd betray Him seven and seventy times over. And even more.'

Vodka and its connotations

Vodka in Russia has a universal value, making it almost a hard currency in its own right. Paying unskilled labourers in vodka instead of money is an accepted, albeit unauthorised, convention. Vodka can also be used in circumstances where the repayment of a loan with money might be inappropriate, impolite or even insulting; to 'put down' vodka is a token of deep respect. Unlike money, which is considered 'dirty', alcoholic beverages have no improper connotations. The superstition that money brings bad luck is common. Passing money hand-to-hand should be avoided, it should be placed instead on a wooden surface to expunge its evil.

Vodka can also be used as a punishment – a 'penalty' or forfeit for losing an argument or bet. This Russian tradition was employed by Czar Peter the Great, who used the 1.5-litre Great Eagle Cup to exact retribution. According to Selmer Fougner in his 1934 *Anthology of Wine and Spirits*: 'When Peter the Great was aboard the ship, everyone had to address him Herr Schout-bij-Nacht. Anyone who failed to do so was to drain the Cup of the Great Eagle. Poor Julius once had the misfortune of forgetting to address the czar in such a manner, but when on Peter's command he was presented with the Eagle, he ran and, scared, climbed atop one of ship's masts. The czar, then, held the Cup with his teeth… and followed the disobedient Julius all the way to the top… As a punishment, he made him drain five Eagles altogether.'

Drinking vodka is the bedrock of many rituals: weddings, wakes, holidays, house-warming parties, seeing someone off on military service, the sexual consummation of a new relationship (as the saying goes, 'there are no ugly women – only not enough vodka'), the beginning ('can't start without a bottle') or ending of a job ('to celebrate', 'if you don't drink to it, it'll perish'). Vodka is used to sanctify oaths, a small glass is allocated to a fallen soldier, it is poured on the ground to protect from dangerous obstacles, it is used to celebrate the birth of a child. The act of drinking can change the status of a non-ritual activity into a ritual: 'If there's a drink, we'll find an occasion.' Far more than simply alcohol, vodka is a sociopolitical, monumental entity.

Vodka can give any conversation special status: 'Looks like it's a regular vicious circle. "Dusia," I tell her, "don't cry. We can't get to the bottom of this without a half-a-litre. I'll go get it. Will be right back"' (Aleshkovsky). Similarly, conversations arising between drinkers are suffused with importance: 'When drunk, you don't do little things. Nobody notices the little things in life. A drunkard in Russia thinks in eternal, cosmic categories. Trivial matters concern him not.' (Yerofeyev: *Moscow-Petushki*). Even complicated public issues might be addressed while drinking strong spirits, as Ivan Pryzov noted in *History of Taverns in Russia in Connection with the History of the Russian People* (2009): 'Any secular affair began, without fail, with a feast or carouse. For this reason, drinks played a crucial cultural role in people's social lives… The inn – call it whatever you wish – a pub or a tavern, was the place for people's gatherings, a people's clubhouse.'

Death and resurrection

Drinking etiquette permits the demonstration of the unpleasant sensations caused by alcohol. Sniffing, snivelling, hiccuping, grunting and burping all indicate that the drinker has enough strength to suppress the need to be sick. This aesthetic of disgust cultivates a singular affinity for all things unpleasant. In *Moscow-Petushki* the protagonist downs a drink then gives the reader an account of his method of suppressing the urge to vomit: 'I started to strangle myself.' The superseding of one set of unpleasant sensations by another is a reinterpretation of the etiquette of dignity. A popular joke runs:

'A nobleman wakes up in the morning with a severe hangover. He moans, holds his head between his hands, rocks from side to side, but can't bring himself to drink a hair of the dog.

"Oh, I feel so bad… so bad," he says.

Then he calls his servant. "Vaska! Bring the cat over here!"

"Meow!"

"Now, start twisting his balls."

"MEOW! MEOW! MEOW!"

Finally, the nobleman has a drink. "Phew! Yeah, he didn't like that".'

This affinity for the unpleasant seems to be connected with a love of death, as in Vladimir Shinkarev's cult 1980 novel *Maxim and Fyodor*: 'I would even go so far as give the same definition to binge drinking – learning to die.' Indeed, alcoholic intoxication is often described as a kind of death or struggle with mortality, as in the lyrics of Vystotosky:

> 'Some drank till they died,
> But in fact they didn't; they lived…'

If extreme levels of drunkenness are linked to death, then sobering up is a rebirth: 'It's all right, Yerofyev… Talitha kum [I say to you, arise], as your Queen said when you were lying in the coffin.' According to Boris Levin and Jussi Simpura's *Demystifying Russian Drinking: comparative studies from the 1990s*, 'A hangover coupled with an inability to have a drink is akin to death, a crucifixion; drinking a hair of the dog brings with it yet another resurrection.' In both literature and folklore, drinking hard spirits can be interpreted not only as mortifying the flesh, as a duel with a drinking companion or even as fighting the 'green serpent' or dragon, but as imbibing the magical water that heals wounds and brings the dead back to life.

The idea of drink-as-death is linked to the ritual ingestion of poisons practised by the Persian king, Mithridates VI (135–63 BCE), who regularly took sub-lethal doses to develop his immunity. As a result, he survived a suicide attempt, finally begging his servant to kill him with a sword. Comparing drunkards directly or indirectly to Mithridates recurs frequently in Russian literature, as in *Moscow-Petushki*, whose narrator fails to commit suicide despite ingesting lethal doses of alcohol and is finally stabbed to death.

The usual drinking toasts are 'to health', 'to wealth' and 'to sexual prowess' ('I drink to money and a hard-on!'). Other toasts are more restrained, almost akin to spells: 'To us!', 'May it always be so!', 'We are alive as long as we are not dead'. As early as the 17th century Olearius noted that drinking toasts had acquired magical connotations – toasts to the prince, for instance, wished him 'good luck, victories, health, and so that there remains no more blood in his enemies than wine in this cup.' The protagonist of *Moscow-Petushki* even wishes that someone could come up with a recipe for a cocktail that 'one can, without remorse, drink in the presence of God… in His name,' suggesting it might be called 'River of Jordan', to put it in the same category as Holy Water. Traditionally, however, the beverage drunk in the name of God is wine, an ancient symbol of fecundity identified with human blood even before Jesus Christ took wine and pronounced: 'For this is my blood'.

Drinking is often described in terms that invoke the solemnity of a rite. For instance, in *Moscow-Petushki* there are no friendly parties (there are no friends and the narrator's drinking companions are are assembled at random), no carousing (nobody is actually drunk), no civilised evenings (characters drink for days on end), no easy-going gatherings. Alcohol is scarce and comes from unanticipated sources because no one has any money; there are no feasts because there is no food. Instead, the action described within the narrative is much closer to ritual. According to Russian custom, during a wake a shot of vodka and a small amount of food are set aside for the deceased. In *Moscow-Petushki* the narrator is reminiscent of Jesus Christ or Lazarus because he constantly faces imminent death or death seems already to have taken him. Events begin to resemble the deceased drinking at his own wake, or a requiem for his suicide.

Russian drinking traditions can hardly be understood from a logical or rational perspective. Even the greatest Russian philosophers and writers could not explain why their compatriots drink with such selfless heroism. In his 1890 essay 'Why do Men Stupefy Themselves?', Leo Tolstoy writes: 'Ask anyone why he began drinking wine and why he now drinks it. He will reply, "Oh, I like it, and everybody drinks," and he may add, "it cheers me up." Some – those who have never once taken the trouble to consider whether they do well or ill to drink wine – may add that wine is good for the health and adds to one's strength; that is to say, will make a statement long since proved baseless… [Yet] the use of these evidently harmful things produces terrible evils known and admitted by everyone, and destroys more people than all the wars and contagious diseases added together. And people know this, so they cannot really use these things just "to while away the time".'

Fyodor Dostoyevsky in *A Writer's Diary* (covering most of the 1870s) observes: 'In what way can demon-vodka resemble the courier? It can do so very easily in the way it coarsens and brutalises a man, makes him callous, turns him away from clear thinking and desensitises him to the power of goodness. A drunkard doesn't care about kindness to animals; a drunkard will abandon his wife and children. A drunken man came to the wife he had abandoned and whom, along with his children, he had not supported for many months; he demanded vodka and set to beating her to force her to give him still more vodka.'

The notion that the origins of drinking stem from poverty and sorrow, that people drink to avoid a tragic and unbearable reality, to forget their unhappiness and misfortunes, has its origins in 19th-century literature. Mikhail Gorbachev shared the same naive notion within his *Memoirs* (1996): 'What were the reasons behind people drinking en masse? They were numerous: the hardship that millions of people had to endure, the poor living conditions, the low level of culture… The depressing atmosphere of society compelled weaker individuals to drown their sense of inferiority and fear of the cruel world around them with alcohol.'

Diatribes against alcohol coexist with vindications; along with proverbs and sayings that stigmatise drink are as many that sing its praises. The latter assure us that God himself gave us wine, that it brings beatitude ('Wine makes your heart happy'), repose ('There's nothing better than an old friend and some old wine'), performs miracles ('A barrel of wine can perform more miracles than a church full of saints'), gives us strength ('Bread revitalises you, wine makes you stronger'), rectifies misfortunes ('Wine is the cure of all adversities'), washes away life's agonies ('Wine is the remedy for sorrows'), imparts intelligence and power ('There is wisdom in wine, strength in beer, and germs in water') and even brings light ('Wine is the light in the darkness of life'). Consuming alcohol in large quantities can also help us to discover subconscious depths within ourselves, as articulated by poet Igor Guberman (b. 1936):

> 'Wine takes me to the depths of me,
> Where when sober I can never be.'

Indeed, the notion that alcohol expands consciousness is widespread. From this viewpoint, intoxication is considered to be a meta-state, encompassing all other states and revealing levels of reality that would otherwise be inaccessible. Getting drunk beomes a means of measuring and uncovering the depths of the mind.

In reality, the rich in Russia drink no less than the poor; the educated drink in the same way as the uneducated; drinking 'in joy' is as prevalent as drinking 'in sorrow'; and drinking to 'expand' one's mind happens as often as drinking to neutralise it, or simply to render yourself unconscious. As much as a drunk can 'find' himself and his true essence, he can also 'lose' himself and all things human.

Both those who damn alcohol and those who extol it often view 'drinking' independently of its cultural context, or offer hazy mythological explanations for its power. These modern 'myths' simply obstruct our ability to reflect.

Photographs: Vladimir Sichov. Moscow and Vladimir, mid-1970s.

RUSSIAN SERIES

Russian Criminal Tattoo Encyclopaedia Volume I, Danzig Baldaev and Sergei Vasiliev
ISBN: 978-0-9558620-7-6

Russian Criminal Tattoo Encyclopaedia Volume II, Danzig Baldaev and Sergei Vasiliev
ISBN: 978-0-9550061-2-8

Russian Criminal Tattoo Encyclopaedia Volume III, Danzig Baldaev and Sergei Vasiliev
ISBN: 978-0-9550061-9-7

Russian Criminal Tattoo Police Files Volume I, Arkady Bronnikov
ISBN: 978-0-9568962-9-2

Russian Criminal Tattoo Police Files Volume II, Arkady Bronnikov
ISBN: 978-0-9931911-2-1

Drawings from the Gulag, Danzig Baldaev
ISBN: 978-0-9563562-4-6

Soviets, Danzig Baldaev and Sergei Vasiliev
ISBN 978-0-9568962-7-8

Soviet Space Dogs, Olesya Turkina
ISBN: 978-0-9568962-8-5

Home-Made: Contemporary Russian Folk Artifacts, Vladimir Arkhipov
ISBN: 978-0-9550061-3-5

Notes from Russia, Alexei Plutser-Sarno
ISBN: 978-0-9550061-7-3

CCCP COOK BOOK, Olga and Pavel Syutkin
ISBN: 978-0-9931911-1-4

Soviet Bus Stops, Christopher Herwig
ISBN: 978-0-9931911-0-7

Published in 2017

Murray & Sorrell FUEL Ltd
FUEL Design & Publishing
33 Fournier Street
London E1 6QE

fuel-design.com

Images © FUEL Publishing
Photographs © Vladimir Sichov
Essays © Alexei Plutser-Sarno
Co-ordinated by Julia Goumen
Translated by Ast A. Moore, GnMTranslations.com

Distribution by Thames & Hudson / D. A. P.
ISBN 978-0-9931911-5-2
Printed in China